PRAISE FOR *HOW TO THINK*

"Absolutely splendid … Jacobs's emphasis on the relational nature of thinking is essential for understanding why there is so much bad thinking in political life right now." *New York Times*

"This may not be the most uncivil political era of all time, Jacobs argues, but there's something about it that is distinctively terrible … How to Think is part essay, part lament, part how-to guide for processing the world more generously." *Atlantic*

"Wise and delightful …" *Wall Street Journal*

"Refreshing and hopeful, even as it points out some of our worst habits of 'not thinking' … this book is a guide in how you should hold positions, and how you should regard and interact with those of a fundamentally different mind." *Paris Review* (Staff Pick)

"Witty, engaging, and ultimately hopeful, Jacobs's guide is sorely needed in a society where partisanship too often trumps the pursuit of knowledge." *Publishers Weekly*

"Just when it feels like we've all lost our minds, here comes Alan Jacobs's How to Think, a book infused with the thoughtfulness, generosity, and humor of a lifelong teacher. A mindful book for our mindless times." Austin Kleon, author of *Steal Like an Artist*

ALAN JACOBS is the Distinguished Professor of the Humanities at Baylor University. He has written extensively for The Atlantic, WSJ, The New Atlantis, and Harper's and is the author of several books including a well-received biography of C. S. Lewis and a book on the pleasures of reading. Find him on *twitter.com/ayjay* and visit his website at *http://blog.ayjay.org/*

ALSO BY ALAN JACOBS

The Narnian: The Life and Imagination of C. S. Lewis (2005)

Original Sin: A Cultural History (2008)

The Pleasures of Reading in an Age of Distraction (2011)

The Book of Common Prayer: A Biography (2013)

HOW TO THINK

A GUIDE FOR THE PERPLEXED

ALAN JACOBS

PROFILE BOOKS

This paperback edition published in 2018

First published in Great Britain in 2017 by
PROFILE BOOKS LTD
3 Holford Yard
Bevin Way
London
WCIX 9HD

www.profilebooks.com

First published in the United States of America in 2017 by
Convergent Books, an imprint of the Crown Publishing Group,
a division of Penguin Random House LLC

10 9 8 7 6 5 4 3 2

Printed and bound in Great Britain by
CPI Group (UK) Ltd, Croydon CRO 4YY

A CIP catalogue record for this book is available from the British
Library.

ISBN 978 1 78125 957 3
eISBN 978 1 78283 406 9

To the students and faculty of the Honors College at
Baylor University

CONTENTS

HOW TO
THINK

INTRODUCTION

Why we're worse at thinking than we think

"What were you *thinking*?" It's a question we ask when we find someone's behavior inexplicable, when we can't imagine what chain of reasoning could possibly lead to what they just said, or did. But even when we're not at the point of exasperation, we can still find ourselves wondering where our friends and family and neighbors got such peculiar ideas. And it might even happen, from time to time, in the rare quiet hours of our lives, that we ask how we got our own ideas—why *we* think the way we do.

Such matters strike me as both interesting and important: given the questions that constantly confront us as persons and societies, about health and illness, justice and injustice, sexuality and religion, wouldn't we all benefit from a better understanding of what it means to think well? So in the past few years I've read many books about thinking, and while they offer varying and in some cases radically incompatible models of what thinking is, there's one trait all of them share: they're *really* depressing to read.

They're depressing because even when they don't agree on anything else, they provide an astonishingly detailed and wide-ranging litany of the ways that thinking goes astray— the infinitely varied paths we can take toward the seemingly inevitable dead end of Getting It Wrong. And these paths to error have names! Anchoring, availability cascades, confirmation bias, the Dunning-Kruger effect, the endowment effect, framing effects, group attribution errors, halo effects, ingroup and outgroup homogeneity biases, recency illusions . . . that's a small selection, but even so: what a list. What a chronicle of ineptitude, arrogance, sheer dumbassery. So much gone wrong, in so many ways, with such devastating consequences for selves and societies. Still worse, those who believe that they are impeccably thoughtful turn out to be some of the worst offenders against good sense.*

So surely, I think as I pore over these books, it's vital for me (for all of us) to get a firm grip on good thinking and bad, reason and error—to shun the Wrong and embrace the Right. But given that there appear to be as many kinds of

---

*Some of the books that chronicle these errors will be referred to throughout this book. The most important one is Daniel Kahneman's *Thinking, Fast and Slow* (Farrar, Straus and Giroux, 2011). I will also cite Jonathan Haidt's *The Happiness Hypothesis: Finding Modern Truth in Ancient Wisdom* (Basic Books, 2005) and *The Righteous Mind: Why Good People Are Divided by Politics and Religion* (Pantheon, 2012). Also useful is Dan Ariely's *Predictably Irrational: The Hidden Forces That Shape Our Decisions* (HarperCollins, 2008; 2nd ed., 2012). But you can also take a shortcut to thoroughgoing despair simply by reading the Wikipedia page called "List of Cognitive Biases."

mental error as stars in the sky, the investigation makes me dizzy. After a while I find myself asking: What are these people even talking about? What, at bottom, *is* thinking?

THINKING IN ACTION: AN EXAMPLE

Imagine that you and your partner are buying a car. You're not a pure impulse buyer, so you're not going to choose on appearance alone (unless, of course, a car is so hideously ugly that you'd be ashamed to be seen in it). You know that there are many factors to keep in mind, and you try to remember what they all are—gas mileage, reliability, comfort, storage space, seating, sound system. Do we need extra features, like a GPS?, you might ask. How much more would it cost to have that installed?

A checklist helps, but it's not going to tell you which items on the list should have greater priority and which less. Maybe you'd say in general that comfort is more important than gas mileage, but what if the car's an absolute guzzler? That could be a deal breaker.

Anyway, here you are at the used car lot. This blue Toyota looks nice, and the reviews on the major websites are positive. You look it over, you sit in it and consult your lumbar region: Everything feel pretty good down there? You take it for a test drive and it seems to you that the ride is a little rough, though it could be that you're paying *too much* attention and have made yourself oversensitive, like the princess in "The Princess and the Pea." You try to factor in that possibility.

You go through this ritual three or four times and then you make your decision, which you're relatively pleased with until you get home and your partner comments that the *obviously* best choice would have been the one you ruled out at the beginning because you thought it looked hideous, at which point you reflect that maybe you shouldn't have tried to make this decision on your own.

This is what thinking is: not the decision itself but what goes into the decision, the consideration, the assessment. It's testing your own responses and weighing the available evidence; it's grasping, as best you can and with all available and relevant senses, what *is,* and it's also speculating, as carefully and responsibly as you can, about what *might be.* And it's knowing when not to go it alone, and whom you should ask for help.

The uncertainties that necessarily accompany predicting the future—not only do you not know what will happen but you don't even know how you'll *feel* about what happens, whether you'll eventually stop noticing that uncomfortable seat or will want to drive the car off a cliff because of it—mean that thinking will always be an art rather than a science. (Science can help, though; science is our friend.)

My father had an almost unerring ability to buy bad cars, for a simple reason: He never actually thought about it. He acted always on impulse and instinct, and his impulses and instincts, like mine and yours, weren't very reliable. But he *liked* acting impulsively, and I believe he would rather have owned a lousy car than devoted research and planning to the task of purchasing one. (Verily, he had his reward.) But I was always annoyed with him because it seemed obvious to me that buying a decent automobile isn't that hard. Yes, no matter what you do, you *can* end up with a lemon, but with due diligence you dramatically reduce the likelihood of that happening. It's a matter of observing the percentages and refusing to heed your immediate impulses—a bit like playing poker, in that respect.

The problem is, as things-we-think-about go, buying a car is one of the simpler and more straightforward cases. It contains all the key elements, but it's considerably less complicated than the issues and questions—political, social, religious—that really befuddle us and set us at odds with our fellow residents of this vale of tears. If everything we have to think about were as easy as buying a car, then I'd need only to write a blog post or a few tweets to set us all on the right path. Instead, I've had to write this book.

SPEED KILLS

A few years ago, the eminent psychologist Daniel Kahneman summarized a lifetime of research into cognitive error in a big book called *Thinking, Fast and Slow,* and near the end of that book he came around to the really central question: "What can be done about biases? How can we improve judgments and decisions, both our own and those of the institutions that we serve and that serve us?"

To which he replies: "The short answer is that little can be achieved without a considerable investment of effort." Well, that's fine; after all, we'd all be happy to invest a great deal of effort to rid ourselves of biases that deform our thinking, would we not? But as Kahneman continues, the news gets worse. A considerable part of our thinking apparatus, the part that generates our immediate intuitions, "is not readily educable. Except for some effects that I attribute mostly to age, my intuitive thinking is just as prone to overconfidence, extreme predictions, and the planning fallacy as it was before I made a study of these issues." This is not encouraging.

It is perhaps presumptuous of me to think that I can offer a more hopeful picture than the great Daniel Kahneman, but I truly believe that there are some insufficiently explored ways to understand and ameliorate the problems we have in thinking. We have thought too much in recent years about the science of thinking and not enough about the art. There are certain *humanistic* traditions, some of them quite ancient, that can come to our aid when we're trying to think about thinking, and to get better at it.

But it would be foolish to neglect what people like Kahneman have studied and learned. In the passage I just quoted, he talks about "intuitive thinking": this is the "fast" kind. It's what provides us with snap judgments, instantaneous reads on a given situation, strong predispositions toward approving some ideas and disapproving others. Kahneman calls this System 1, and says that it is supplemented and sometimes corrected by System 2, which is conscious reflection. We go through life basically running System 1; System 2 kicks in only when we perceive a problem, an inconsistency, an anomaly that needs to be addressed. This is why another psychologist who has researched thinking, Jonathan Haidt, uses a different set of terms when he's describing essentially the same distinction: he thinks of intuitive thinking as an elephant, and conscious decision-making as the rider. The idea is that our intuitive thinking is immensely powerful and has a mind of its own, but can be gently steered—by a rider who is truly skillful and understands the elephant's inclinations. It's a hopeful image, and indeed Haidt is more cheerful about the possibility of better thinking than Kahneman is.

In this book I will be writing largely about the rider rather than the elephant, System 2 rather than System 1. I will certainly draw a great deal from major scholars like Kahneman and Haidt, and several others, but I will also suggest that they do not always frame our problems with thinking in the most useful and constructive ways. In particular I'm going to argue that we go astray when we think of our task primarily as "overcoming bias." For me, the fundamental problem we have may best be described as an orientation of the *will*: we suffer from a settled determination to avoid thinking. Relatively few people *want* to think. Thinking troubles us; thinking tires us. Thinking can force us out of familiar, comforting habits; thinking can complicate our lives; thinking can set us at odds, or at least complicate our relationships, with those we admire or love or follow. Who needs thinking?

Moreover, conscious thinking is, as Kahneman indicates in his book's title, *slow*. Jason Fried, the creator of the popular project-management software Basecamp, tells a story about attending a conference and listening to a talk. He didn't like the talk; he didn't agree with the speaker's point of view; as the talk went on he grew more agitated.

When it was over, he rushed up to the speaker to express his disagreement. The speaker listened, and then said: "Give it five minutes."*

Fried was taken aback, but then he realized the point, and the point's value. After the first few moments of the speaker's lecture, Fried had effectively stopped listening: he had heard something he didn't agree with and immediately entered Refutation Mode—and in Refutation Mode there is no listening. Moreover, when there is no listening there is no *thinking*. To enter Refutation Mode is to say, in effect, that you've already done all the thinking you need to do, that no further information or reflection is required.

Fried was so taken by the speaker's request, he adopted "Give it five minutes" as a kind of personal watchword. It ought to be one for the rest of us too; but before it can become one, we should probably reflect on the ways that our *informational habits*—the means (mostly online means) by which we acquire and pass on and respond to information— strongly discourage us from taking even that much time. No social-media service I know of enforces a waiting period before responding, though Gmail allows you to set a delay in sending emails, a delay during which you can change your

---

* https://signalvnoise.com/posts/3124-give-it-five-minutes. In *The Righteous Mind* (p. 81) Haidt reports on an experiment conducted at Harvard in which people were asked to make a moral judgment on a particular issue—but some were not allowed to register their judgments until two minutes had elapsed. This delay allowed people to do a better job of recognizing poor arguments, arguments whose flaws were not as readily seen by those who were allowed to respond immediately. In thinking, it appears, every minute helps.

mind and "unsend." However, the maximum delay allowed is thirty seconds. (Twenty-four hours might be more useful.)*

Does it seem to you that I'm exaggerating the problem? Or just blaming social media? Could be. But as soon as I read Fried's anecdote I realized that I too am regularly tempted to enter Refutation Mode—and the more passionate I feel about a topic, the more likely I am to succumb to that temptation. I know what it's like to become so angry at what someone has written online that my hands shake as they hover over the keyboard, ready to type my withering retort. Many are the tweets I wish I could take back; indeed many are the tweets I have actually deleted, though not before they did damage either to someone else's feelings or to my reputation for calm good sense. I have said to myself, *If I had just thought about it I wouldn't have sent that.* But I was going with the flow, moving at the speed of the social-media traffic.

Maybe you're confident that you're not like that. But before you dismiss the possibility, why don't you just give it five minutes?

---

*A former Google employee named Tristan Harris is attempting to persuade software engineers to stop trying to take advantage of users in this way, to stop what he calls the "race to the bottom of the brain stem." Bianca Bosker, in a story in the November 2016 issue of *The Atlantic* called "The Binge Breaker," quotes Harris: "You could say that it's my responsibility" to back away from the phone, "but that's not acknowledging that there's a thousand people on the other side of the screen whose job is to break down whatever responsibility I can maintain." Harris wants those software engineers to adopt a kind of "Hippocratic oath" not to be so exploitative of users' cognitive wiring. "There is a way to design based not on addiction." Whether engineers will follow that better way . . . I'm not holding my breath waiting.

CONSENSUS AND EMOTION

It could be coincidence, or synchronicity, or fate; but some-times there's a blessed convergence between what you read and what you need. A few months ago I happened to be reading, for unrelated reasons, essays by two wise writers, Marilynne Robinson and T. S. Eliot. And I happened to be reading them at a moment when I was undertaking a serious reassessment of the time I was spending online, especially on social media. That was when the idea for this book began to coalesce in my mind.

In a 1994 essay called "Puritans and Prigs," Robinson challenges the contemptuous attitudes many people have toward the Puritans—the very word is no more than an in-sult now—and gives a more generous and accurate account of what they thought and why they thought it. In the writ-ing of the essay it occurred to her that "the way we speak and think of the Puritans seems to me a serviceable model for important aspects of the phenomenon we call Puritan-ism." That is, the kinds of traits we label "puritan"—rigidity, narrowness of mind, judgmentalism—are precisely the ones people display whenever they talk about the Puritans.*

And why is this? Why are people so puritanical about the Puritans? "Very simply," Robinson writes, "it is a great example of our collective eagerness to disparage without

---

*Marilynne Robinson, "Puritans and Prigs," in *The Death of Adam: Essays on Modern Thought* (Houghton Mifflin Harcourt, 1999), pp. 150–73.

knowledge or information about the thing disparaged, when the reward is the pleasure of sharing an attitude one knows is socially approved." That is, we deploy the accusation of Puritanism because we know that the people we're talking to will share our disparagement of Puritanism, and will approve of us for invoking it. Whether the term as we use it has any significant relationship to the reality of Puritan actions and beliefs is totally irrelevant. The word doesn't have any *meaning* as such, certainly not any historical validity; it's more like the password to get into the clubhouse.

Robinson further comments that this kind of usage "demonstrates how effectively such consensus can close off a subject from inquiry," which may be the most important point of all. The more useful a term is for marking my inclusion in a group, the less interested I will be in testing the validity of my use of that term against—well, against any kind of standard. People who like accusing others of Puritanism have a fairly serious investment, then, in knowing as little as possible about actual Puritans. They are invested, for the moment anyway, in *not thinking*.

Robinson's analysis is acute, and all the more so given that it was written before the Internet became a culturewide phenomenon. Why would people ever think, when thinking deprives them of "the pleasure of sharing an attitude one knows is socially approved"—especially in an online environment where the social approval of one's attitudes is so much easier to acquire, in the currency of likes, faves, followers, and friends? And to acquire *instantaneously*?

Robinson concludes this reflection with the sobering

comment that in such an environment "unauthorized views are in effect punished by incomprehension," not because we live in a society of conscious and intentional heresy hunters, though to some extent we do, "but simply as a consequence of a hypertrophic instinct for consensus." If you want to think, then you are going to have to shrink that "hypertrophic instinct for consensus." But given the power of that instinct, it is extremely unlikely that you, dear reader, are willing to go to that trouble.

That instinct for consensus is magnified and intensified in our era because we deal daily with a wild torrent of what claims to be information but is often nonsense. Again, this is no new thing. T. S. Eliot wrote almost a century ago about a phenomenon that he believed to be the product of the nineteenth century: "When there is so much to be known, when there are so many fields of knowledge in which the same words are used with different meanings, when everyone knows a little about a great many things, it becomes increasingly difficult for anyone to know whether he knows what he is talking about or not." And in such circumstances—let me add emphasis to Eliot's conclusion—*"when we do not know, or when we do not know enough, we tend always to substitute emotions for thoughts."**

This is another idea that seems more incisive as a diagnosis of our time than of its own. And it dovetails

---

*T. S. Eliot, "The Perfect Critic," in *The Sacred Wood: Essays on Poetry and Criticism* (1920), pp. 9–10. Note that the problem, for Eliot, is not that emotions are involved, but that they *substitute for* thought, that they *replace* thinking. Later on we'll explore the vital role of emotion in thinking.

disturbingly with Robinson's analysis. People invested in not knowing, not thinking about, certain things in order to have "the pleasure of sharing an attitude one knows is socially approved" will be ecstatic when their instinct for consensus is gratified—and wrathful when it is thwarted. (Social bonding is cemented by shared emotion, shared emotion generates social bonding. It's a feedback loop from which reflection is excluded.) Between them, Robinson and Eliot explain a great deal about the constant frantic *agita* of life online—and, increasingly I think, offline.

Anyone who claims not to be shaped by such forces is almost certainly self-deceived. Human beings are not built to be indifferent to the waves and pulses of their social world. For most of us the question is whether we have even the slightest reluctance to drift along with the flow. The person who genuinely wants to think will have to develop strategies for recognizing the subtlest of social pressures, confronting the pull of the ingroup and disgust for the outgroup. The person who wants to think will have to practice patience and master fear.

BELONGING TO MULTIPLE COMMUNITIES

I believe I can help those who want to think better, but—I need to say it before taking one more step—no, it's not because I'm an academic. My fellow academics, taken as a group, are just as reluctant to engage in genuine reflection as the less highly educated person in the street. Academics have always been afflicted by unusually high levels of conformity to expectations: one of the chief ways you prove yourself worthy of an academic life is by getting very good grades, and you don't get very good grades without saying the sorts of things that your professors like to hear.*

So, again, no: academic life doesn't do much to help one think, at least not in the sense in which I am commending thinking. It helps one to amass a body of knowledge and to learn and deploy certain approved rhetorical strategies, which requires a good memory, intellectual agility, and the like. But little about the academic life demands that you question your impulsive reactions—and that's true, as Daniel Kahneman suggests, even when what you do with your academic life is study impulsive reactions.

Being a *teacher,* though: that's a different thing. I have been teaching undergraduates for more than thirty years now, and generally speaking undergraduate education is a wonderful laboratory for thinking. Most of my students know what they believe, and want to argue for it, but they also realize that they still have a lot to learn. (The widespread belief that college students are unteachably arrogant know-it-alls does not match my experience. I know the type, but it's not a common one, and it's not any more common now than it was when I started this game.) It's very rewarding to

---

* As Jeff Schmidt writes in *Disciplined Minds* (Rowman & Littlefield, 2001), academia and the other high-ranking professions are good at maintaining "ideological discipline" within their ranks, and people who do well in the academy tend to have "assignable curiosity," which is to say, they are obediently interested in the things they're told to be interested in.

show them not necessarily that their beliefs are wrong, but that they haven't defended them very well, haven't understood their underlying logic, haven't grasped the best ways to commend their views to skeptical Others.* I estimate that in my time I have graded about fifteen thousand student essays, which means that I have seen *all* the ways an argument can go right and *all* the ways one can go wrong.

But as valuable as that long experience has been in thinking about thinking, still more valuable has been my participation in multiple communities that are often at odds with one another. I am an academic, but I am also a Christian. When I hear academics talk about Christians, I typically think, *That's not quite right. I don't believe you understand the people you think you're disagreeing with.* And

---

*This is perhaps a good place to say that it was teaching freshman writing classes that got me thinking about thinking for the first time. I taught such classes for around twenty years, and came to rely heavily on the good old *Norton Reader,* an anthology of essays meant to help such writers. It has gone through a great many changes over the years: I started using it when it was in its third edition, and as I write these words it's in its fourteenth. (It'll probably be in the twenties by the time you *read* these words.) Some of the essays I relied on most heavily in my first years of teaching—William Golding's "Thinking as a Hobby," Annie Dillard's "Seeing" (an excerpt from *Pilgrim at Tinker Creek*), William G. Perry, Jr.'s "Examsmanship and the Liberal Arts"—have fallen by the wayside over the decades, though Orwell's "Politics and the English Language" remains. Reading those essays with my students, trying to get them to apply those writers' insights to their own work, consistently *failing* to get them to apply those writers' insights to their own work—all this was my best education in thinking. I remain grateful to the editors for their wonderfully rich gathering of essays.

when I listen to Christians talk about academics I have precisely the same thought. I have spent decades noting these pervasive misunderstandings, trying to figure out how they arise, and looking for ways to correct them.

Thirty years ago, when the anthropologist Susan Friend Harding began seriously to study American fundamentalist Christianity—study that eventuated in a remarkable account, *The Book of Jerry Falwell: Fundamentalist Language and Politics*—she discovered that her colleagues were deeply suspicious of her interests: Why would someone want to investigate such weird and obviously unpleasant people? "In effect," Harding wrote, "I am perpetually asked: Are you now or have you ever been a born-again Christian?" Many readers will recognize Harding's sly echo of the question posed to hundreds of people by the House Un-American Activities Committee in the 1950s: "Are you now or have you ever been a Communist?"*

In 1991 Harding published a powerful essay on this phenomenon. Aren't anthropologists, she asked, intrinsically interested in cultural structures and practices that are different from their own? Why, then, were so many of them repelled by the idea of studying such difference when the difference lived right next door, and could vote in the same elections the anthropologists voted in? The title of Harding's essay is "Representing Fundamentalism: The Problem of the

---

*Susan Friend Harding, *The Book of Jerry Falwell: Fundamentalist Language and Politics* (Princeton University Press, 2000). The essay I quote in the following paragraph is "Representing Fundamentalism: The Problem of the Repugnant Cultural Other," *Social Research* 58, no. 2 (Summer 1991): 373–93.

Repugnant Cultural Other," and the phrase *repugnant cultural other* is one that we will have cause to employ in the pages to come. In fact, it will turn up so often that we'd best give it an initialism: RCO.

As I hinted earlier, if fundamentalist or evangelical Christians tend to be the RCO for secular academics, the reverse is true as well—and that mutual suspicion is something I've been trying to navigate my whole adult life. And now I live in a political order that, taken as a whole, has assumed the lamentable traits—willful incomprehension, toxic suspicion—that I'm used to seeing in those smaller mutually antagonistic communities. Everyone today seems to have an RCO, and everyone's RCO is on social media somewhere. We may be able to avoid listening to our RCO, but we can't avoid the realization that he or she is there, shouting from two rooms away.

This is a profoundly unhealthy situation. It's unhealthy because it prevents us from recognizing others as our neighbors—even when they are quite literally our neighbors. If I'm consumed by this belief that that person over there is both Other and Repugnant, I may never discover that my favorite television program is also his favorite television program; that we like some of the same books, though not for precisely the same reasons; that we both know what it's like to nurse a loved one through a long illness. All of which is to say that I may all too easily forget that political and social and religious differences are not the whole of human experience. The cold divisive logic of the RCO impoverishes us, all of us, and brings us closer to that primitive state that the political philosopher Thomas Hobbes called "the war of every man against every man."

We can do better; we *should* do better. And I believe, thanks in part to my years of negotiating mutually hostile communities, I can help. I know what it's like to make common cause with people who are in some ways alien to me; I know how such experiences can expand my understanding of the world; I know how they can force me to confront the narrowness of my vision and my tendency to simplistic thinking—sometimes to not thinking at all. And, with apologies to Daniel Kahneman, I really do believe that I've gotten considerably better at thinking over the years. And I don't want to keep what I've learned to myself.

OBLIQUE STRATEGIES

Much of what follows will be simply *diagnostic,* and there's a good reason for that. Once, years ago, I started having chest pains, and my doctors couldn't isolate the problem: I exercised regularly, my heart seemed healthy, nothing was evidently wrong. But the pains kept coming back, and that scared me. Finally, one doctor asked some probing questions and discovered that I had had, before the pains began, a lingering heavy cough. It seemed that coughing had strained a muscle in my chest, and that was the source of the pain; and when I started worrying about it, the resulting anxiety tensed the muscle and increased the pain—which then led to more anxiety. It was the classic vicious circle of reinforcement. When I asked the doctor what treatment he thought best, he replied, "The diagnosis *is* the treatment. Now that you know you don't have a life-threatening illness, you won't worry so much, and less stress in your mind will mean less stress on your chest muscles. That'll give them a chance to heal." Similarly, while I will offer positive prescriptions in the pages to come, simply *knowing* the forces that act on us to prevent genuine reflection, making an accurate diagnosis of our condition, is the first course of treatment.

Beyond that: I would love to offer you a set of invariable instructions that you could follow step by step to become a better thinker, but thinking isn't like that. Again, while science is our friend, thinking is fundamentally an art, and art is notoriously resistant to strict rules—though there are good practices to follow, and I will describe those practices in the pages to come. (Indeed, I've already hinted at almost all of them in describing the buying of an automobile.) But whoever it was who first said that happiness is something one cannot aim straight at, but rather can achieve only by focusing on other good things, could have said it about thinking and been equally correct.

Back in 1975 the musician Brian Eno and the artist Peter Schmidt created a curious artifact, a set of cards containing peculiar instructions: "Honour thy error as a hidden intention." "Ask your body." "Work at a different speed." These were meant to help artists, especially musicians, who had come to an impasse in their work. Eno and Schmidt called the card deck Oblique Strategies because they knew that when an artist is blocked, direct approaches meant to fix the problem invariably make it worse. In a similar way, sometimes you can get better at thinking only by turning your attention to matters other than thinking. So what follows will be sometimes anecdotal, sometimes circuitous—but eventually we will always circle back to the forms that bad thinking takes, and discover habits that can help us better practice this most delicate of arts. It won't be easy; that's part of the point. But we can do this.

one

BEGINNING TO THINK

*Why it wouldn't be a good idea to think
for yourself, even if you could*

A few years ago Megan Phelps-Roper, a member of Westboro Baptist Church in Topeka, Kansas, a church founded by her grandfather Fred Phelps, decided to start using Twitter to spread the Westboro message. That message might be summed up by the statement most closely associated with WBC: God Hates Fags. (The church registered the URL godhatesfags.com all the way back in 1994.) As Adrian Chen reports in his *New Yorker* profile of Phelps-Roper, Twitter was a perfect venue for getting this kind of message across, thus this typical Phelps-Roper tweet: "Thank God for AIDS! You won't repent of your rebellion that brought His wrath on you in this incurable scourge, so expect more & worse!"*

---

*The story of Megan Phelps-Roper is brilliantly told by Chen in his article for the November 23, 2015, issue of *The New Yorker*, "Unfollow." Everything I know about the situation I learned from Chen's article.

But there was something Phelps-Roper didn't anticipate: on Twitter, people talk back to you. When she began tweeting at a Jewish web developer named David Abitbol—"Oh & @jewlicious? Your dead rote rituals == true repentance. We know the diff. Rev. 3:9 You keep promoting sin, which belies the ugly truth"—Abitbol responded with bemused humor. He would later comment that "I wanted to be like really nice so that they would have a hard time hating me." This kind of response threw Phelps-Roper off-balance. As she later told Adrian Chen, "I knew he was evil, but he was friendly, so I was especially wary, because you don't want to be seduced away from the truth by a crafty deceiver."

We're probably all subject to what the literary critic Gary Saul Morson calls "backshadowing"— "foreshadowing after the fact," that is, the temptation to believe that we can look into the past and discern some point at which the present became inevitable. ("I should have seen it coming!")* But it's hard not to think that by engaging with Abitbol in a friendly way Phelps-Roper had already set off down the road that would lead her away from Westboro Baptist Church. She started responding to others who shared Abitbol's skepticism about her beliefs, and some of them also proved funny, or interesting, or kind. She told Chen, "I was beginning to see them as human," instead of as the faceless RCO.

But it was the relationship with Abitbol—they even met in person, ironically enough, when Phelps-Roper picketed a

---

*Gary Saul Morson, *Narrative and Freedom: The Shadows of Time* (Yale University Press, 1994), chap. 6.

gathering that Abitbol had helped to organize—that mattered more than any other. And that relationship became so decisive for Phelps-Roper largely because Abitbol took the trouble to look into what Westboro members believed and why they believed it. They claimed to base their views that homosexuality should be punished by death on the Bible, particularly Leviticus 20:13: "If a man lies with a male as with a woman, both of them have committed an abomination; they shall surely be put to death; their blood is upon them." But wait a minute, Abitbol said: Didn't Jesus say, when a woman was found to have committed adultery, that the "one without sin" should cast the first stone at her? And, by the way, didn't Megan's own mother have an illegitimate son, the product of an affair she had had in law school? Shouldn't *she* "surely be put to death"?

Phelps-Roper knew, and deployed, the standard Westboro response: that gays and lesbians attended Gay *Pride* parades—they were *proud* of their sins—whereas her mother had repented. To which Abitbol replied: How can gays and lesbians ever repent if you kill them?

To this Phelps-Roper had no ready answer, and when she asked leaders of Westboro, they had none either. Phelps-Roper had already realized that believing in the Bible didn't necessarily require her to perform the hostility that most members of Westboro exemplified. (When questioned about her friendliness to unbelievers she replied by citing Proverbs 25:15. "By long forbearing is a prince persuaded, and a soft tongue breaketh the bone.") But now Abitbol was asking deeper and harder questions, not about whether the Bible was true, but rather about whether her community really bothered to discern and obey what they claimed was their supreme authority in all matters.

Phelps-Roper's response to this crisis in her mental history is fascinating and extremely telling. She took two actions. First, while she continued to go picketing with other Westboro members, she stopped carrying the signs that read "DEATH PENALTY FOR FAGS"; and second, she ceased her correspondence with David Abitbol.

This twofold response perfectly embodies the mental state of the person who has *begun to think*. She didn't leave the church, she didn't stop picketing; but she drew a line in her own mind that had the inevitable effect of separating her, to some degree, from the community which until that point had given meaning to her whole life.

Which helps to explain why she took the second step: ending communication with Abitbol. On some level, if not consciously, Phelps-Roper had to have known that that one issue—DEATH PENALTY FOR FAGS—was unlikely to be the end of the story. If Westboro was wrong about that, then what else might they be wrong about? If the answer turned out to be "a lot," then the result could be exile from the only world she had ever known, the only belonging she had ever experienced. So she closed the door from which she perceived the greatest threat.

But it was too late; and there were many other doors, as long as she engaged with different sorts of people online. In the end exile was Megan Phelps-Roper's fate.

LOSING A PLACE IN THE WORLD

Stories of forbidden knowledge come in many varieties, but in our time this is one of the more common: the tale of a community that provides security in exchange for thought, and the courageous member of that community who, daring to think, sacrifices the security. It's the Enlightenment—whose rallying cry is, Immanuel Kant said, *Sapere aude!*—dare to think, dare to be wise—writ small and writ in a hundred ways. Perhaps the canonical example today is Lois Lowry's *The Giver,* that favorite of middle school teachers everywhere, with its rather blunt leading metaphor of moving from the monochromaticism of the protagonist's little world to the Technicolor variety of the world outside. A more complex treatment of the theme may be found in Aldous Huxley's *Brave New World,* where one of the major characters, Bernard Marx, sees through the stultifying conformity of *his* society but does so not through audacity but through psychological maladjustment.

But when I think of Megan Phelps-Roper, whose story isn't finished yet, whose final verdict on her upbringing in Westboro Baptist Church has not been made and may never be made definitively, the story that comes to my mind is Ursula K. Le Guin's "The Ones Who Walk Away from Omelas." Le Guin tells us of a utopia built on a single (but perpetual) act of cruelty, and of those who, once they face that cruelty, find that they can no longer dwell within their perfect city. But Le Guin does not tell us of the beautiful Technicolor world that they enter when they leave Omelas; nor does she describe anything like the Savage Reservation that Huxley offers as a radical counterpart to the main-stream society of his drug-fueled "brave new world." Rather, she gives us this:

> They leave Omelas, they walk ahead into the darkness, and they do not come back. The place they go towards is a place even less imaginable to most of us than the city of happiness. I cannot describe it at all. It is possible that it does not exist. But they seem to know where they are going, the ones who walk away from Omelas.*

This ending deprives us of the easy comforts that *Sapere aude* stories tend to offer—the reassurance that, though life in the bigger world may be hard at times, may even be miserable, it is nonetheless the right trade to make because the security of community is not really the most vital thing in the long run. Le Guin's swerve from the more familiar form of the trope says: We don't know that. To *think,* to dig into the foundations of our beliefs, is a risk, and perhaps a tragic risk. There are no guarantees that it will make us happy or even give us satisfaction.

WHY THINKING FOR YOURSELF IS IMPOSSIBLE

I'd bet a large pile of cash money that thousands of people read Adrian Chen's profile of Megan Phelps-Roper and said,

---

* In Le Guin's collection *The Wind's Twelve Quarters* (Harper & Row, 1975), pp. 283–84.

to others or to themselves, "Ah, a wonderful account of what happens when a person stops believing what she's told and learns to *think for herself.*" But here's the really interesting and important thing: that's not at all what happened. Megan Phelps-Roper didn't start "thinking for herself"—she started thinking *with different people.* To think independently of other human beings is impossible, and if it were possible it would be undesirable. Thinking is necessarily, thoroughly, and wonderfully social. Everything you think is a response to what someone else has thought and said. And when people commend someone for "thinking for herself" they usually mean "ceasing to sound like people I dislike and starting to sound more like people I approve of."

This is a point worth dwelling on. How often do we say "she really thinks for herself" when someone rejects views that *we* hold? No: when someone departs from what we believe to be the True Path our tendency is to look for bad influences. She's fallen under the spell of so-and-so. She's been reading too much *X* or listening to too much *Y* or watching too much *Z.* Similarly, people in my line of work always say that we want to promote "critical thinking"—but really we want our students to think critically only about what they've learned at home and in church, not about what they learn from *us.**

---

*See Patrick Deneen's wonderful essay "Critical Thinking About Critical Thinking": http://patrickdeneen.blogspot.com/2008/11/thinking-critically -about-critical.html. I might also pause to note here that one of my least favorite rhetorical practices is use of what I call the "false we": When people say things like "We need to learn to be more tolerant of difference," what they typically mean is "*You* need to learn to

When we believe something to be true, we tend also to see the very process of arriving at it as clear and objective, and therefore the kind of thing we can achieve on our own; when we hold that a given notion is false, we ascribe belief in it to some unfortunate wrong turning, usually taken because an inquirer was led astray, like Hansel and Gretel being tempted into the oven by a wicked witch. And yet even the briefest reflection would demonstrate to us that nothing of the sort is the case: there is no connection between independence and correctness, or social thinking and wrongness.

Jean Piaget, the great child psychologist—or, as he preferred to call himself, "genetic epistemologist"—tells a wonderful story about two little boys. (He doesn't say so, but I expect that they were his own children.) One night when the moon was full, the older, who was about four, led his younger brother into the front garden of his house and ordered him to walk back and forth. As little brother faithfully did so, big brother carefully observed him—and the moon. "I was trying to see if the moon follows him when he walks," the older brother explained. "But it doesn't, it only follows me."*

---

be more tolerant of difference." When in the paragraph above I say that "we" academics want our students to be critical only about what they've learned from other people, I can't help acknowledging that I am as guilty of that sin as anyone else in my profession. So I had to use "we" there; and I do so in a few other places as well, where my conscience won out over my dislike of a rhetorical tic.

*Jean Piaget, *Play, Dreams, and Imitation in Childhood* (Norton, 1962).

What an exemplary instance of the truly scientific mind at work! Big brother first formed an original hypothesis and then devised an experiment to test the hypothesis. Given the limits of his knowledge, it was a beautifully designed experiment, with a clear result. His conclusions were half-wrong (he correctly determined that the moon did not follow his little brother); but they were the product of genuine, and genuinely impressive, thought. By contrast, if he had been told that a giant had hung the moon in the sky as a great lamp to guide his nocturnal hunting, and had believed that tale, he would rightly have understood that the moon doesn't follow anyone. But the correctness of the conclusion would not erase the falsity of the premises.

This should not in any way lessen our admiration for the boy's ingenuity; but it should remind us that all of us at various times in our lives believe true things for poor reasons, and false things for good reasons, and that whatever we think we know, whether we're right or wrong, arises from our interactions with other human beings. Thinking independently, solitarily, "for ourselves," is not an option.

ON REASON AND FEELING (DIVIDED OR JOINED)

While we're clearing away misconceptions about thinking, let's tackle another pervasive one: that in order to think well, one must be strictly rational, and being rational requires the suppression of all feelings.* Here we'd do well to look at

---

*A brief historical digression: If you consider the character of these

the story of another person, not a Christian American of our time but an English philosopher and religious skeptic named John Stuart Mill.

Mill's autobiography recounts how his father educated him, and one may get the flavor of the plan by reading one of the book's first sentences: "I have no remembrance of the time when I began to learn Greek; I have been told that it was when I was three years old."* James Mill believed that children were capable of learning far more, and learning it far earlier, than almost anyone else believed. He made his eldest son the test case for his conviction, and in many respects quite a successful test case: after all, John Stuart Mill became more famous, more influential, and more highly regarded as a thinker than his father.

Mill confesses that being raised in this peculiar manner was sometimes difficult. He makes no mention of his mother in the *Autobiography,* and little mention of his siblings, except to note that he became their teacher. The shadow of his father seems to have blocked out almost everything else. In a kind of summary passage, Mill comments that "the element which was chiefly deficient in his moral relation to his children was that of tenderness." He did not blame his father for

---

two misconceptions—the value of thinking for yourself and the necessity of eliminating feelings from the rational act—you can see how much of our common understanding of thinking is derived from one work, René Descartes's *Meditations on First Philosophy* (1641), in which Descartes describes himself sitting alone in a hot kitchen with a piece of paper in his hand and asks how he can *know* that he's sitting alone in a hot kitchen with a piece of paper in his hand.
* Mill wrote his *Autobiography* in the last months of his life, and it was published after his death in 1873.

this: "He resembled most Englishmen in being ashamed of the signs of feeling, and, by the absence of demonstration, starving the feelings themselves."

But how does the younger Mill judge the experiment that was performed on him—the experiment that in a sense he *was*? "As regards my own education, I hesitate to pronounce whether I was more a loser or gainer by his severity." Again, in many respects James Mill's experiment was a rousing success. His eldest son became a figure on London's intellectual stage when he was still in his teens, and James Mill had good reason to believe that John Stuart would be a great force for the social reform that both of them believed was desperately needed in England. But it was just at this point of promise-about-to-be-realized, in 1826, when Mill was twenty years old, that he confronted what he called "a crisis in my mental history." (The attentive reader will note that I used a parallel phrase in describing Megan Phelps-Roper.) Mill sums up his crisis in this way:

It occurred to me to put the question directly to myself: "Suppose that all your objects in life were realized; that all the changes in institutions and opinions which you are looking forward to, could be completely effected at this very instant: would this be a great joy and happiness to you?" And an irrepressible self-consciousness distinctly answered, "No!" At this my heart sank within me: the whole foundation on which my life was constructed fell down. All my happiness was to have been found in the continual pursuit of this end. The end had ceased to charm, and how could there ever again be any interest in the means? I seemed to have nothing left to live for.

Mill kept this collapse to himself—as, in effect, he had been taught by his father to do. ("He resembled most Englishmen in being ashamed of the signs of feeling.") In perhaps the most heartbreaking passage in his account Mill comments, "I sought no comfort by speaking to others of what I felt. If I had loved anyone sufficiently to make confiding my griefs a necessity, I should not have been in the condition I was." He lived this way for months, mechanically laboring at the East India Company, where he worked, of course, for his father, and wondering how long he could survive in such a condition. "I generally answered to myself that I did not think I could possibly bear it beyond a year."

Over time he managed to get a little better—not healed, not happy, but functional—no longer in constant imminent danger of collapse. And then something curious happened to him: in the autumn of 1828, he picked up a book of poems by William Wordsworth, and for the first time in a long time felt something like *delight*. And this delight had the effect of reinvigorating his will.

James Mill had focused his energies relentlessly on developing his son's analytical and critical powers, and had seen no place for poetry in that scheme. But what the younger Mill in his misery came to see was the disturbing truth that "the habit of analysis has a tendency to wear away the feelings . . . when no other mental habit is cultivated, and the analysing spirit remains without its natural complements and correctives." And the wearing away of feelings was a great and complex loss.

The analytical mind constantly separates, divides, distinguishes, until its whole mental world lies in pieces around it. And where will that mind acquire the energy it needs to put things back together? In the aftermath of his collapse and poetic restoration, Mill writes, "The cultivation of the feelings became one of the cardinal points in my ethical and philosophical creed." But what did the cultivation of the feelings actually *do*? And what did it do for *thinking*?

One of Mill's closest friends at that time was a man named John Arthur Roebuck. Roebuck became his chief antagonist in debates on these matters—though not because he scorned poetry; in fact, "he was a lover of poetry and of most of the fine arts." What, then, was the point of disagreement? Simply that "he never could be made to see that these things have any value as aids in the formation of character." Instead, Roebuck found that his own feelings got in his way:

> He saw little good in any cultivation of the feelings, and none at all in cultivating them through the imagination, which he thought was only cultivating illusions. It was in vain I urged on him that the imaginative emotion which an idea, when vividly conceived, excites in us, is not an illusion but a fact, as real as any of the other qualities of objects.

With that quotation we're ready to grasp Mill's argument—and why it matters for our little project here. Mill's defense of the feelings and the imagination has two components. The first is that bringing analytical power to bear on a problem is not enough, especially if one's goal is to make the world a better place. Rather, one must have a certain kind of *character*: one must be a certain kind of person, a person who has both the ability and the inclination to take the products of analysis and reassemble them into a positive account, a structure not just of thought but also of feelings that, when *joined to* thought, can produce meaningful action.

The second component is this: when your feelings are properly cultivated, when that part of your life is strong and healthy, then your responses to the world will be *adequate* to what the world is really like. To have your feelings moved by the beauty of a landscape is to respond to that landscape in the way that it deserves; to have your feelings moved in a very different direction by the sight of people living in abject poverty is to respond to *that* situation in the way that it deserves. The latter example is especially relevant to someone like Mill who wishes to be a social reformer: if your analysis leads you to the conclusion that is it unjust that people suffer in poverty in a wealthy country, but your feelings do not match your analysis, then something has gone awry with you. And it may very well happen that if the proper feelings are not present and imaginatively active, then you will not even bother to do the analysis that would reveal unmistakable injustice. If the feelings are not cultivated the analytical faculties might not function *at all*. (This is a point to which we will return.)

It is, then, for John Stuart Mill, looking back from the end of his life on his youthful sufferings, impossible to draw a line that separates analysis on the one side from feeling on the other and to conclude that only the first side is relevant to thinking. The whole person must be engaged, all the faculties present and accounted for, in order for real thinking to take place. Indeed, this for Mill is what it means to *have* character: to be fully alive in all your parts and therefore ready to perceive the world as it is—and to act responsibly toward it.

WILT CHAMBERLAIN'S MANLY RATIONALITY

A move from philosophy to basketball may seem curious, but it will help us add to our understanding of what it means to be rational. Recently I was listening to an episode of Malcolm Gladwell's podcast *Revisionist History* in which he was marveling at human irrationality, as manifested by the famous basketball player Wilt Chamberlain. Gladwell noted that Chamberlain's one great weakness as a basketball player was free-throw shooting, and further noted that only during the brief period in his career when he shot free throws underhanded did his percentage from the charity stripe improve. Why, then, did he go back to shooting in a more conventional but less successful style? Because, Wilt later admitted, he was embarrassed to shoot the ball in a way that might be perceived as girlish or sissy.

How astonishingly irrational! cries Gladwell. To sacrifice success in your vocation because you're afraid of what people might think or say! And then, as is his wont, he goes on to offer an explanation for this bizarre behavior. I don't think it's a very good explanation, but I'll set that aside for now. Instead, I want to unpack his claim that Chamberlain's behavior is irrational, because it rests on an unconfronted assumption. (Many errors in thinking arise from assumptions people don't know they're making.) Gladwell assumes that if Wilt had been thinking rationally, the *only* thing he would have been concerned about was success in his job.

But that's because Gladwell, like many of us, seems to have unwittingly internalized the idea that when professional athletes do the thing they're paid to do, they're not acting according to the workaday necessity (like the rest of us) but rather are expressing with grace and energy their inmost competitive instincts, and doing so in a way that gives them delight. We need to believe that because much of *our* delight in watching them derives from our belief in *their* delight. (In much the same way we enjoy watching the flight of birds, especially big birds of prey, associating such flying with freedom even though birds actually fly from necessity: they need to eat. And yet we have no interest in watching members of our own species drive to McDonald's.)

Many professional athletes have confessed that, while they do sometimes find great satisfaction and even, yes, delight in their work, they never forget that it is indeed work. Many's the night when they take the field or court not for the joy of it but because if they don't they won't get paid. Which is to say that athletes are like the rest of us: they find some degree of value in their work, but work is by no means the only thing they care about. We work for leisure, many of us.

In his leisure time, Wilt Chamberlain had one central interest: having sex with as many women as possible. (He famously claimed in an autobiography to have bedded twenty thousand, which has caused many envious and/or skeptical readers to resort to arithmetical calculation.) This is what Gladwell missed when assessing the rationality of Chamberlain's free-throw shooting. If your primary goal in life is to have sex with as many people as possible, then you very well might avoid any behavior that could lower your reputation for desirability. What if some woman you approach had heard someone say, "Wilt's a great player, I guess, but only a sissy would use that granny shot"? And who knows, perhaps Wilt actually heard the s-word from a woman he was pursuing; that, or something like that, could have influenced him to abandon the far more successful underhand style of free-throw shooting.

Moreover, what was Wilt actually giving up when he returned to a more "manly" style of free-throw shooting? Several points a game, perhaps; but only rarely would that make a difference in the game's outcome. And anyway: when Wilt shot free throws underhanded, he was the most unstoppable force the game of basketball had ever seen; then, when he returned to the conventional method he was . . . *still* the most unstoppable force the game had ever seen. You could say, then, that he gave up little in his workplace in order to create potentially more interesting opportunities for himself in an arena that meant more to him. This kind of decision making may be ethically dubious, but it's anything but irrational.

RELATIONAL GOODS

We might call Gladwell's error the What's the Matter with *What's the Matter with Kansas* Problem. Thomas Frank's 2004 book famously tries to address what is to him an astonishing puzzle: why so many people in the American heartland vote in defiance of their "best interests." But

Frank, like Gladwell, conceives of only one relevant good to be sought: if in Gladwell's tale of Wilt Chamberlain the only excellence that matters is workplace excellence, for Frank the only real "interests" that people have are financial interests. Both writers overlook *relational goods*. In Chamberlain's case the relevant relations are purely sexual—given his numerical ambitions, none of his encounters could have lasted more than a few hours—while the factors for Frank's representative Kansans are, as many critics of the book have noted, communal. (That is, Frank doesn't acknowledge that people might be willing to make economic sacrifices in order to live in societies they think of as morally stronger.) But none of those "other" commitments are any less rational than the desire for economic and workplace success.

As can be seen from these examples, I'm not paying anyone a compliment when I speak of relational goods. Chamberlain's Don Juanism is, in my judgment, both wrong and sad. The "Kansan" desire for communal solidarity is far more noble, though that impulse is sadly subject to its own perversions. My point is simply that an account of rational thinking, and a resulting set of judgments about irrational thinking, that can't account for the power and the value of relational goods is a deeply impoverished model of rationality.

So just as we do not "think for ourselves" but rather think with others, so too we think in active *feeling* response to the world, and in constant *relation* to others. Or we should. Only something that complete—relational, engaged, honest—truly deserves to be called thinking. In a preface to his novel *The Princess Casamassima,* Henry James writes, "But there are degrees of feeling—the muffled, the faint, the just sufficient, the barely intelligent, as we may say; and the acute, the intense, the complete, in a word—the power to be finely aware and richly responsible."* This is thinking: *the power to be finely aware and richly responsible.* We just need to learn how to be more aware, how to act more responsibly.

---

*James, *The Art of the Novel: Critical Prefaces,* ed. Colm Tóibín (University of Chicago Press, 2011), p. 62.

two

ATTRACTIONS

How good people can be led to do bad things

Leah Libresco, of the same generation as Megan Phelps-Roper, grew up on Long Island in a family where atheism was simply assumed. "Religion didn't really rise to the level of plausibility for me to think about denying it as a major part of my identity, any more than 'UFO skeptic' is how anyone would introduce themselves." And this attitude, or perhaps it would be better to say lack of attitude, was common in Libresco's world: in her high school history class studying the Reformation, a classmate raised her hand and asked whether there were still any Lutherans. Leah Libresco is now a Roman Catholic.*

---

*The best starting point for Libresco's story is this interview with *America* magazine: http://americamagazine.org/content/all-things/my-journey-atheist-catholic-11-questions-leah-libresco. It contains links to her posts on the experiences I describe in this chapter. Libresco has recently married and is now known as Leah Libresco Sargeant.

How did this happen? First of all, one might ask whether her parents ever took measures against her being drawn toward theism. One suspects not. Atheists have a tendency to think that atheism is humanity's future, and religious belief an evolutionary leftover that's useless at best and at worst dangerous, like the vermiform appendix; not the sort of thing one needs to make a special effort to protect oneself from. And insofar as Libresco knew, or thought she knew, anything about Christianity, it was American Protestant fundamentalism—something perhaps resembling the theology (if not necessarily the marketing strategy) of Westboro Baptist Church.

So when she came to Yale University and met Catholic and Orthodox Christians—people grounded in an older faith with stronger intellectual buttressing—Libresco did not have ready refutations of their views. But that probably wouldn't have mattered if she hadn't made what proved to be a fateful decision for her: she joined a debating society, the Yale Political Union. It's vital to note that, though many of the people in YPU had experience in competitive debate, that's not what the society did. "At the end of a debate, no one won, and no points were awarded." But in its own way the society was deeply competitive. "When we kept score," Libresco says, "we counted in converts." That is, what really mattered was that you actually *won someone over*—and not to the position you were assigned for the evening, but to something you actually believed in.

Now, it would be more accurate to say that winning someone over was one of the *two* things that really mattered. The other was *being won over*. Members who interviewed for some leadership position in the YPU would usually be asked, "Did you ever break someone on the floor?" To "break on the floor," in the society's parlance, was to change your mind in the middle of a debate, right there in front of everyone. To break someone on the floor was a signal achievement. But— and here is the really essential thing—the candidate would also be asked, "So, have *you* ever broken on the floor?" And to this question, Libresco says, "The correct answer was yes." After all, "It wasn't very likely that you'd walked into the YPU with the most accurate possible politics, ethics, and metaethics. If you hadn't had to jettison some of your ideas several years in, we had our doubts about how honestly and deeply you were engaging in debate." James Boswell, in his famous *Life of Samuel Johnson,* speaks of Johnson's habit of "talking for victory," but in the YPU, at least at its best, this would not be a virtue.

In that sense the stakes in the YPU were considerably higher than the stakes of standard competitive debate: you didn't just win or lose according to what some judges decreed about your ability to defend a designated position; you were vulnerable to changes of your own mind. And changing your mind could yield a different *you.* But the whole ethos of the YPU, in Libresco's experience, was built around the willingness to expose yourself to just such a risk. To be "broken on the floor" was a token of good faith and an indication of a willingness not just to accept but to live out the values of the community. Libresco internalized those values, and that eventually made it possible, or at least easier, for her to embrace a set of beliefs, and a way of life, that set her at odds with her own upbringing.

In the previous chapter I wrote that we always think with others, and Libresco's story illustrates that point. It also suggests that our ability to think well will be determined to some considerable degree by who those others are: what we might call the moral form of our community. A willingness to be "broken on the floor," for example, is in itself a testimony to belief that the people you're debating are decent people who don't want to harm or manipulate you—whereas if you don't trust people you're unlikely to allow them anything like a "victory" over you. This suggests that the problem of belonging and not-belonging, affiliation and separation, is central to the task of learning how to think.

BINDING, BLINDING, AND THE INNER RING

In his 2012 book *The Righteous Mind,* Jonathan Haidt tries to understand why we disagree with one another—especially, but not only, about politics and religion—and, more important, why it is so hard for people to see those who disagree with them as equally intelligent, equally decent human beings.

Central to his argument is this point: "Intuitions come first, strategic reasoning second. Moral intuitions arise automatically and almost instantaneously, long before moral reasoning has a chance to get started, and those first intuitions tend to drive our later reasoning." Our "moral arguments" are therefore "mostly post hoc constructions made up on the fly, crafted to advance one or more strategic objectives."

Haidt talks a lot about how our moral intuitions accomplish two things: they *bind* and they *blind*. "People bind themselves into political teams that share moral narratives. Once they accept a particular narrative, they become blind to alternative moral worlds." "Moral matrices bind people together and blind them to the coherence, or even existence, of other matrices."

But how do we acquire these initial moral intuitions— or, rather, the ones that prove decisive for our moral lives? (I make that distinction because, as we have just seen, people often end up dissenting, sometimes in the strongest possible terms, from the moral frameworks within which they were raised.) Haidt offers a partial answer to this question by contending that people have different genetic predispositions to the new: some of us are *neophilic*, others *neophobic*. But this really isn't a very helpful answer, especially in describing people who change: even a person who does make a major shift will in her lifetime have experienced any number of new ideas, but will have rejected or ignored most of them. So the question remains: What triggers the formation of a "moral matrix" that becomes for a given person the narrative according to which everything and everyone else is judged?

I think C. S. Lewis answered that question in December 1944, when he gave the Commemoration Oration at King's College in London, a public lecture largely attended by students. Lewis called his audience's attention to the presence, in schools and businesses and governments and armies and indeed in every other human institution, of a "second or unwritten system" that stands parallel to the formal organization—an Inner Ring.* The pastor is not always the most influential person in a church, nor the boss in the workplace. Sometimes groups of people with no formal titles or authority are the ones who determine how the organization works. They form its Inner Ring.

Lewis does not think that any of his audience will be surprised to hear of this phenomenon; but he thinks that some may be surprised when he goes on to make this claim: "I believe that in all men's lives at certain periods, and in many men's lives at all periods between infancy and extreme old age, one of the most dominant elements is the desire to be inside the local Ring and the terror of being left outside." And it is important for young people to know of the force of this desire because "of all passions the passion for the Inner Ring is most skillful in making a man who is not yet a very bad man do very bad things."

The draw of the Inner Ring has such profound corrupting power because it never announces itself as evil—indeed, it never announces itself at all. On these grounds Lewis makes a "prophecy" to his audience at King's College: "To nine out of ten of you the choice which could lead to scoundrelism will come, when it does come, in no very dramatic colours. . . . Over a drink or a cup of coffee, disguised as a triviality and sandwiched between two jokes . . . the hint will come." And when it does come, "you will be drawn in, if you are drawn in, not by desire for gain or ease, but simply because at that moment, when the cup was so near your lips,

---

*C. S. Lewis, "The Inner Ring," in *The Weight of Glory and Other Addresses* (HarperOne, 2001), pp. 141–57.

you cannot bear to be thrust back again into the cold outer world."* It is by these subtle means that people who are "not yet very bad" can be drawn to "do very bad things"—by which actions they become, in the end, very bad people.

This, I think, is how our "moral matrices," as Haidt calls them, are formed: we respond to the irresistible draw of belonging to a group of people whom we happen to encounter and happen to find immensely attractive. We may be acting under the influence of strong genetic predispositions, but how those dispositions are activated seems largely to be a matter of what particular people one happens to bump into and when. The element of sheer contingency here is, or ought to be, terrifying: had we encountered a group of equally attractive and interesting people who held very different views, then we too would hold very different views.

Of course, my explanation hasn't taken us very far beyond Haidt's. I might plausibly be accused of saying that people are attracted to the ideas of people they are attracted to. But it's hard to go much further while speaking in a general mode. For some, the attraction of the new people will be that they seem smart; for others, that they're rich, or beautiful. For still others being radically different, socially

---

*In a 2016 article in the *Journal of Applied Social Psychology*, "Going to Extremes for One's Group: The Role of Prototypicality and Group Acceptance" (46:9, September 2016, pp. 544–53), Liran Goldman and Michael A. Hogg demonstrate that people who are uncertain of their place within a group will, more frequently than those who are at the group's center, "go to extremes" to prove their fidelity. We might say that when the cup is so near their lips, they cannot bear to be thrust back again into the cold outer world.

or religiously or politically, from one's immensely annoying family may be key.

But in any case, once we *are* drawn in, and allowed in, once we're part of the Inner Ring, we maintain our status in part by coming up with those post hoc rationalizations that confirm our group identity and, equally important, confirm the nastiness of those who are Outside, who are Not Us. (That's the theme of the next chapter.) And it's worth noting, as Avery Pennarun, an engineer at Google, has commented, that one of the things that makes smart people smart is their skill at such rationalization: "Smart people have a problem, especially (although not only) when you put them in large groups. That problem is an ability to convincingly rationalize nearly anything."*

THE BELONGING WE NEED: MEMBERSHIP

In "The Inner Ring" Lewis portrays this group affiliation in the darkest of terms. That's because he's warning people about its dangers, which is important. But there *are* healthier kinds of group affiliation, and one of the primary ways we can tell the difference between an unhealthy Inner Ring and

---

*From a post on his personal blog: http://apenwarr.ca/log/?m=201407 #01. Pennarun in the same post makes this telling comment: "What I have learned, working here, is that smart, successful people are cursed. The curse is confidence. It's confidence that comes from a lifetime of success after real success, an objectively great job, working at an objectively great company, making a measurably great salary, building products that get millions of users. You must be smart. In fact, you are smart. You can prove it."

a healthy community is by their attitudes toward *thinking*. The Inner Ring discourages, mocks, and ruthlessly excludes those who ask uncomfortable questions. This can be seen most clearly in extreme cases, as, for instance, when people participate in some kind of mass political movement, as Eric Hoffer has explained in his classic study *The True Believer*:

> Thus when the frustrated congregate in a mass movement, the air is heavy-laden with suspicion. There is prying and spying, tense watching and a tense awareness of being watched. The surprising thing is that this pathological mistrust within the ranks leads not to dissension but to strict conformity. Knowing themselves continually watched, the faithful strive to escape suspicion by adhering zealously to prescribed behavior and opinion. Strict orthodoxy is as much the result of mutual suspicion as of ardent faith.

Hoffer goes on to make the incisive point that "the loyalty of the true believer is to the whole—the church, party, nation—and not to his fellow true believer." Indeed, that fellow true believer might be pretending—which *he* also suspects *you* of. For Hoffer, "True loyalty between individuals is possible only in a loose and relatively free society." And this is true on a smaller scale and in less extreme situations as well. The genuine community is open to thinking and questioning, so long as those thoughts and questions come from people of goodwill.*

To explore this contrast further, we'll continue using

---

* Eric Hoffer, *The True Believer: Thoughts on the Nature of Mass Movements* (Harper Perennial, 1951), pp. 124–27.

C. S. Lewis as our guide, because these are matters that he thought about very often and very well. Lewis is of course best known as a Christian thinker and storyteller, but I believe his ideas about our social formation—how we end up inside some groups and outside others—don't owe much to the Christian beliefs he settled on when he was around thirty. Rather, they reach back into his early adolescence, at a time when he had no religious beliefs at all. His understanding of these matters was formed by his experience at a boarding school, where he found himself, as a solitary and bookish child, thrown into a rigidly stratified, hierarchical, and competitive world of boys, in which he was expected to find and maintain a place. He hated every minute of it, and seeing what the survival-of-the-obsequious world did to his peers was surely the origin of his ideas about the Inner Ring.

Only in small ways and on rare occasions was he able to discern some alternative to Inner-Ringery, and years later to write about it, in an address he gave under the title "Membership." The address was given to a meeting of Christians, and its most immediate applications are to the life of the Christian church, but its implications are far, far broader.

Lewis thinks that the modern Western world tends to give us a choice between solitude—not always easy to choose—and "inclusion in a collective," a collective for Lewis being an environment in which we all have more or less the same status and identity: as, for instance, part of the audience at a concert, or the crowd at a football game. What tends to get lost in our world is *membership,* which is neither solitary nor anonymous. Lewis explains:

How true membership in a body differs from inclusion in a collective may be seen in the structure of a family. The grandfather, the parents, the grown-up son, the child, the dog, and the cat are true members (in the organic sense), precisely because they are not members or units of a homogeneous class. They are not interchangeable. Each person is almost a species in himself. . . . If you subtract any one member, you have not simply reduced the family in number; you have inflicted an injury on its structure.

But, Lewis goes on to say, genuine membership can happen in less formal and generally recognized ways—for instance, in a group of friends. He cites as a paradigmatic example the quartet of Rat, Mole, Badger, and Toad from *The Wind in the Willows* (one of his favorite books). They are all so different from one another, made of such dramatically varying stuff, yet taken together they are far greater than the sum of their parts. Each requires the others to be complete. Badger's friends draw him out of his gruff solitude; Toad needs the others to . . . well, to get him out of the trouble he's constantly getting himself into. Without Ratty, Mole would never have learned the pure joy of "messing about in boats."

What is perhaps most important about this quartet is that none of them makes any effort to make another conform to some preestablished mold. No one wants even Toad to change fundamentally, only to exercise a bit more self-restraint. Each is accepted for his own distinctive contribution to the group: if it were less distinctive it would be less valuable. This is also, I might add, the key point about the friendship of Harry, Hermione, and Ron in the Harry

Potter books: there is not a great deal of overlap in their personalities and inclinations except that, being Gryffindors, they are all brave. (It's curious that the examples that come to my mind of this kind of informal membership, sustained by affection and an easy acceptance of idiosyncrasy, tend to be from children's books—perhaps most adults no longer dare to hope for connections like these.)

But for people of all ages, some form of genuine membership is absolutely necessary for thinking. We have already seen that it is not possible to "think for yourself" in the sense of thinking independently of others; and we have likewise seen how the pressures imposed on us by Inner Rings make genuine thinking almost impossible by making belonging contingent on conformity. The only real remedy for the dangers of false belonging is the true belonging to, true membership in, a fellowship of people who are not so much like-minded as like-hearted.

I had been on Twitter for about seven years when I decided that the environment was just too poisoned by snark and mockery and bitterness and (sometimes) sheer hatred for me to be able to tolerate it any longer. And yet I did not want to abandon the genuine, valuable connections I had forged there. So I decided to create a private Twitter account and ask the people whom I most valued to follow me there. I knew I wanted to keep the circle small—fewer than a hundred people—and to confine the group almost completely to people I've met in person, but beyond those two commitments I didn't have any principles of selection in mind. As it turned out, some were Christians, some Jews, some atheists; some academics, some distrustful of the academy; some socialists, some paleoconservatives. Only when I started writing this section of this book did I realize that I had worked from a "principle of selection" after all: I had chosen to interact with people who had very little in common except that I knew—from experience—that they wouldn't write me out of their own personal Books of Life if I said something they strongly disagreed with. That is, I am confident that I am a *member* (in the organic sense) of a curious little online body, and that has been a real encouragement to me. Sometimes I even try out writing ideas on them—typically only a few are able to answer (they have lives), but when they do answer I know it'll emerge from genuine thought, not merely emotional or visceral reaction. These people, again, are not necessarily like-minded, but they are temperamentally disposed to openness and have habits of listening—and in that sense are wonderfully like-hearted.

It's easy to underestimate the value of such connections. Again Eric Hoffer helps. He comments that "the capacity to resist coercion stems partly from the individual's identification with a group. The people who stood up best in the Nazi concentration camps were those who felt themselves members of a compact party (the Communists), of a church (priests and ministers), or of a close-knit national group." For a twenty-first-century person with a smartphone as well as for the prehistoric hunter-gatherer on the savanna, isolation is deadly, while genuine solidarity is life-giving. The problem that arises for us, as opposed to our hunter-gatherer forebears, is the need to distinguish between "genuine solidarity" and participation in an Inner Ring.

ASSESSING YOUR INVESTMENTS (AND YOUR LEVELS OF OPTIMISM)

In trying to make such a distinction, the first thing that's required, as Socrates told us long ago, is a bit of self-knowledge. And the variety of self-knowledge that's especially valuable here is knowledge of your own personal investments.

A couple of years ago I started corresponding with Christopher Beha, an editor at that venerable American institution *Harper's Magazine,* about whether I might write an article on the decline of the Christian intellectual in America. This possibility was profoundly attractive to me: *Harper's* is, after all, one of the most prestigious of American periodicals, and not one where I'd expect to see a long and detailed reflection on Christianity in America, written by a Christian. So I made every effort to present my ideas in a way that would be attractive and convincing to Chris, and to the other editors there.

But I also thought, *Don't sell yourself out.* I didn't think I would actually lie about what I think to get into the pages of *Harper's,* but there are ways to be dishonest that fall short of actual lying. You can stress certain points more than you believe, in your heart of hearts, they really deserve; you can gently steer your mind away from genuine convictions that might prove too controversial. Now, I could tell myself that I was simply striving to match my writing to my audience, which is a necessary and a good thing, yes? Yes. But every good thing can be taken too far. And where is the line that separates (a) matching my writing to my audience from (b) telling people what they want to hear so that I can get into the pages of an influential magazine? I didn't know where the line was—I still don't know where the line is—but I know it exists.

In the end, the article appeared, and I feel pretty good about it; but when I think about it, I can hear a little voice piping from the deep recesses of my skull: *Did you speak your heart's truth? Or did you merely seek to please?* Self-knowledge is hard.

Self-knowledge, though vital, is only part of this story about membership and Inner Rings. If Roger Scruton is right in his book *The Uses of Pessimism,* then one of the impediments to genuine membership is what he calls "unscrupulous optimism." This attitude—it's one of the modes of Hoffer's True Believing—is based on the belief that "the difficulties and disorders of humankind can be overcome by some large-scale adjustment: it suffices to devise a new arrangement, a new system, and people will be released from their temporary prison into a realm of success." (Scruton calls it "unscrupulous" because it lacks scruples, hesitations, self-critical inquiry. It runs headlong.)

Optimistic attempts to promote what is Clearly Right will be presented as a pursuit of the common good, but Scruton believes that the attitude underlying them is always "I"-based: it's for the good of *me* and people whose views are generally indistinguishable from mine. To this "I" attitude Scruton contrasts the "we" attitude—not the most felicitous phrasing, I think, but the contrast is valuable. The genuine "we" recognizes limits and constraints, boundaries that we cannot transgress and that create the frame that gives meaning to our lives. Moreover, it stands back from the goals of the "I," is prepared to renounce its purposes, however precious, for the sake of the long-term benefits of love and friendship. It takes a negotiating posture towards the other and seeks to share not goals but constraints. It is finite in ambition and easily deflected; and it is prepared to trade increases in power and scope for the more rewarding goods of social affection.*

What I find especially fascinating about this passage is the way it links a preference for "love and friendship" with "a negotiating posture towards the other." Scruton believes that if we're less concerned with ruling the world than with having a secure place to enjoy the "goods of social affection," then we'll be more likely to treat generously others who want to enjoy those same goods, even if those people are very different from us in both belief and practice.

Now, Scruton is a very traditionalist sort of conservative—he is a longtime defender of fox hunting, for instance—and it must be acknowledged that the argument he makes here can easily be used to prop up an unjust social order. After all, if you're a member of the ruling class, it's very much in your interests to say, "Now, now, let's put aside your selfish interest in having your own way and just enjoy one another's company. Let's take a *negotiating* posture toward one another, shall we?" Such counsel leaves the world as it

---

* Roger Scruton, *The Uses of Pessimism* (Oxford University Press, 2010), p. 17.

is, and disarms demands for justice. So for those who speak on behalf of the oppressed or marginalized, strong *solidarity* is far more important than "keeping an open mind" or "trying to understand the other side" or even being generous to people who are unlike you.

Let's agree with them. Let's place solidarity above open-mindedness, and agree that our deepest convictions need not be always open to scrutiny. (We will see later on that keeping an open mind is only sometimes a good thing.) Even so, there are still many questions that might arise, and should arise, if people were to give a higher priority than they commonly do to thinking.

SOLIDARITY, FRIEND AND FOE

As an example of what I mean, let me reflect on the controversy in 2014 over Ta-Nehisi Coates's ambitious and detailed article for *The Atlantic* "The Case for Reparations." Soon after the article came out, I was discussing it with some friends. We all agreed that it is a very powerful portrayal of a grossly unjust social order, but I commented that as moving as the essay was, I didn't think Coates had actually made a *case* for reparations, in spite of the title. To this statement some of my friends replied: "How could you read that article and not think that those people deserve reparations?"

I answered it wasn't a matter of what they *deserve*: Lord knows they *deserve* more and better than they're ever going to get. I tried to make a distinction between diagnosis and treatment: someone might be accurately diagnosed with cancer, but chemotherapy might not be the best treatment for him, and if I questioned the appropriateness of chemotherapy in a particular case, it would make no sense to accuse me of saying that the patient didn't deserve treatment. Similarly, I could think that black Americans are suffering unjustly from legal and social afflictions whose roots are hundreds of years deep and still not be sure that reparations are the correct remedy. Before I could be sure about that, I needed to have answers to three questions: Who gives? Who receives? Who decides?

I don't think my friends accepted the validity of my argument. But whether I was right or wrong, I think the whole situation raises a vital question involving *ends* and *means*. As I understand the way the conversation unfolded, my friends allowed their unreserved, passionate, and wholly justified endorsement of the ends of Coates's essay—its hope of breaking racism's apparent death grip on the economic and social prospects of black Americans—to shunt aside serious reflection on the *means* of addressing this seemingly permanent affliction at the heart of American life.

They were moved, I think, by a heartfelt commitment to solidarity, and again, at times solidarity should trump what I have called "critical reflection." When your friend has just fallen and broken her arm, it is time to comfort her and get her care, not to offer a lecture on the dangers of skateboarding. That should come later, and perhaps shouldn't come from you at all (depending on what your relationship is). But when Coates makes a "case for reparations," that's a matter of national public policy, which means that, though solidarity with the victims of injustice is an indispensable driver of meaningful political action, solidarity is not enough: it must be supplemented by a colder-eyed look at what particular strategies and tactics are most likely to realize the desired end.

But it's hard to see things that way when you are something of an optimist, in Scruton's sense: a questioning of your preferred means can look like indifference toward your most treasured ends. We all fall into this trap from time to time. But the distinction between the two is absolutely vital, and must always be kept in the forefront of our minds in any public debate. If we are willing to grant, at the outset, that the people we're debating agree about ends—that they want a healthy and prosperous society in which all people can flourish—then we can converse with them, we can see ourselves as genuine members of a community. And even if at the end of the day we have to conclude that we all do *not* want the same goods (which can, alas, happen), it is better that we learn it at the end of the day than decide it before sunrise. Along that path we can learn from one another in a great many ways—and we have a chance of discovering unexpected opportunities for *membership*: for there can be more genuine fellowship among those who share the same disposition than among those who share the same beliefs, especially if that disposition is toward kindness and generosity.

Such networks of affiliation are complicated, and discerning their presence requires what the ancients called "prudence," a virtue that, like many virtues, is cultivated largely by avoiding certain vices: the kind of optimism that Scruton calls "unscrupulous" and its accompanying rushes to judgment, its reluctance to question its preferred means. Prudence doesn't mean being uncertain about what's right; it means being scrupulous about finding the best means to get there, and it leads us to seek allies, however imperfect, in preference to making enemies. And all this matters if we want to think well. As the Bible says, "The simple inherit folly: but the prudent are crowned with knowledge."

three

REPULSIONS

Why you're probably not as tolerant of others as you think

A couple of years ago, Scott Alexander, one of the most consistently thoughtful bloggers active today, and one I read precisely because he helps me think, wrote a post titled "I Can Tolerate Anything Except the Outgroup." In it he set out to answer a question: How is it that straight white men (for example) can be gracious and kind to lesbian black women (for example) while being unremittingly bitter toward other straight white men? What has happened here to the old distinction between ingroups and outgroups? Alexander's answer is that "outgroups may be the people who look exactly like you, and scary foreigner types can become the ingroup on a moment's notice when it seems convenient."*

He then gives a powerful example. He mentions being

---

* http://slatestarcodex.com/2014/09/30/i-can-tolerate-anything-except-the-outgroup/

chastised by readers when he expressed relief that Osama bin Laden was dead. More than one person Alexander found reasonable and thoughtful manifested "conspicuous disgust that other people could be happy about [Bin Laden's] death. I hastily backtracked and said I wasn't happy per se, just surprised and relieved that all of this was finally behind us."

But when Margaret Thatcher died, Alexander continues, "on my Facebook wall—made of these same 'intelligent, reasoned, and thoughtful' people—the most common response was to quote some portion of the song 'Ding Dong, The Witch Is Dead.' Another popular response was to link the videos of British people spontaneously throwing parties in the street, with comments like 'I wish I was there so I could join in.' From this exact same group of people, not a single expression of disgust or a 'c'mon, guys, we're all human beings here.'" And even when he pointed this out, none of his readers saw a problem with their joy in Thatcher's death.

And that's when Alexander realized that "if you're part of the Blue Tribe, then your outgroup isn't al-Qaeda, or Muslims, or blacks, or gays, or transpeople, or Jews, or atheists—it's the Red Tribe." The real outgroup, for us, is the person next door.*

---

*"Post-Partisanship Is Hyper-Partisanship," http://slatestarcodex. com /2016/07/27/post-partisanship-is-hyper-partisanship/. "We think of groups close to us in Near Mode, judging them on their merits as useful allies or dangerous enemies. We think of more distant groups in Far Mode—usually, we exoticize them. Sometimes it's positive exoticization of the Noble Savage variety (understood so broadly that our treatment of Tibetans counts as an example of the trope). Other times it's negative exoticization, treating them as cartoonish stereotypes of evil who are more funny or fascinating than repulsive.

PUNISHING THE OUTGROUP

Since Alexander wrote that initial post, an article has appeared based on research that confirms his hypothesis. "Fear and Loathing Across Party Lines: New Evidence on Group Polarization," by Shanto Iyengar and Sean J. Westwood, indicates that Americans today do not simply *feel* animus toward those who disagree with them politically; they are increasingly prepared to *act* on it. Iyengar and Westwood's research discovers a good deal of racial prejudice, which is to be expected and which is likely to grow worse in the coming years, but people seem to think that they shouldn't be racists or at least shouldn't show it. Not so, when the difference has to do with ideology: "Despite lingering negative attitudes toward African Americans, social norms appear to suppress racial discrimination, but there is no such reluctance to discriminate based on partisan affiliation."* That is, many Americans are happy to treat other people unfairly if those other people belong to the alien Tribe. And—this is perhaps the most telling and troubling finding of all—their desire to punish the outgroup is significantly stronger than their desire to support the ingroup. Through a series of games, Iyengar and Westwood discovered that "outgroup animosity is more consequential than favoritism for the ingroup."

Take Genghis Khan—objectively he was one of the most evil people of all time, killing millions of victims, but since we think of him in Far Mode he becomes fascinating or even perversely admirable—'wow, that was one impressively bloodthirsty warlord.' "

* The article appeared in the *American Journal of Political Science* 59, no. 3 (July 2015).

I mentioned at the outset of this book that many of its themes and topics arise from my belonging to two often antagonistic communities, academia and the Christian church. And of course academia and the church have their own internal antagonisms, which are curiously similar. One phenomenon common to both is the power of the logic usually summed up as "the enemy of my enemy is my friend." People who can't stand one another will form powerful alliances if by doing so they can thwart their ideological enemies—and they will pursue that thwarting with a vigor and resourcefulness that would arouse Napoleon's envy— and with a relentlessness that might well make him quail.

Here we might recall the "unscrupulousness," the headlong rush forward, of the optimists Roger Scruton critiques. When you believe that the brokenness of this world can be not just ameliorated but *fixed,* once and for all, then people who don't share your optimism, or who do share it but invest it in a different system, are adversaries of Utopia. (An "adversary" is literally one who has turned against you, one who blocks your path.) Whole classes of people can by this logic become expendable—indeed, it can become the optimist's perceived *duty* to eliminate the adversaries. As a nineteenth-century pope notoriously commented, "Error has no rights." Caught up by the momentum of his or her cause, the Optimist can easily forget the vital addendum to the papal statement made by Orestes Brownson: "Error has no rights, but the man who errs has equal rights with him who errs not."*

---

*It was Pius IX who made this statement in his famous *Syllabus of Errors* (*Syllabus Errorum,* 1864). Brownson—who was a fervent

One of my consistent themes over the years—one I will return to in this book—has been the importance of acting politically with the awareness that people who agree with you won't always be in charge. That is, I believe that it is reasonable and wise, in a democratic social order, to make a commitment to what political philosophers call *proceduralism*: an agreement that political adversaries ought to abide by the same rules, because this is how we maintain a peaceable social order. That belief is on its way to being comprehensively rejected by the American people. And I have seen this in both academic and ecclesial settings as well: using the existing rules against your opponents, or formulating new ones with the explicit purpose of marginalizing them, without pausing to ask whether such methods are fair, or even whether they might be turned against *you* someday, when the political winds are blowing in a different direction. Such is the power of sheer animus: it disables our ethical *and* our practical judgment.

The task of this chapter is to suggest ways of recognizing the power of animus and strategies for overcoming it. One of the classic ways to do this is to seek out the best—the smartest, most sensible, most fair-minded—representatives of the positions you disagree with. If your first thought on reading that sentence is that smart, sensible, and fair-minded people are extremely rare among your opponents, I would ask you to reflect on whether you think they are any more common among those who agree with you. And if you say they are, then I would encourage you

---

Catholic convert—made his statement in an essay titled "Reform and Reformers" (1863), which was part of the international conversation that led up to Pius's *Syllabus*.

to reflect on one of the lessons of the previous chapter: You have a large emotional investment in thinking that.

We'll discuss some of the ways we could figure out who counts as a "typical" representative of a position, and how important that is; but my chief mission in the latter part of this chapter will be to show you how to find the people who are really worth reading or hearing—even when you disagree with them.

"But," someone may well be saying right about now, "you write as though finding some people and some ideas repulsive is always wrong, intrinsically wrong. But there are some ideas, some points of view, that genuinely are repulsive—and the people who hold them, especially if they hold them vigorously, can be pretty damned repulsive too. Remember GOD HATES FAGS? DEATH PENALTY FOR FAGS?"

Indeed. And yet, as we've seen in our look at the transformation of Megan Phelps-Roper, at least one person who once carried those banners pretty clearly wasn't a monster. And it's highly likely that the number of non-monsters holding monstrous views is greater than one. Over the years, I've had to acknowledge that some of the people whose views on education appall me are more devoted to their students than I am to mine; and that some of the people whose theological positions strike me as immensely damaging to the health of the church are nevertheless more prayerful and charitable, more *Christlike,* than I will ever be. This is immensely disconcerting, even when it doesn't mean that those people are right about those matters we disagree on. Being around those people forces me to confront certain truths about myself that I would rather avoid; and that alone is reason to seek every means possible to constrain the energies of animus.

BULVERISM AND SEA LIONS

What to do when a non-monster holds ideas that strike you as being repulsive—not just wrong, but so repellent that your instinct is to get away as far as possible? Some years ago Leon Kass wrote about what he called the "wisdom of repugnance," and while that concept tends to be associated with conservatism, in point of fact people across the political spectrum believe in the wisdom of repugnance. They just feel repugnance for different kinds of people and different acts.*
I think it's fair to say that our repulsion glands don't secrete their chemical cocktails with complete reliability: sometimes we're rightly repulsed; sometimes we're repulsed unnecessarily, and can learn to get over it. So without denying that there genuinely *is* a wisdom in repugnance, I'm going to focus on those cases when we need to ignore that gland's secretions.

So we have a problem: this person's beliefs are disgusting; this person seems to be just a person. Okay, so maybe he isn't a *monster* as such, but that doesn't mean that he's not seriously messed up: morally corrupted (a "hater") or in the grip of some kind of psychological affliction ("fearful," "angry," "bitter"). Note the embedded assumption in such statements: that error results from pathology. He couldn't be wrong if he weren't morally or psychologically seriously dysfunctional—that's the implicit or explicit message.

And yet all of us have been wrong. People you love and

---

*Kass's essay "The Wisdom of Repugnance" (*New Republic,* June 2, 1997) focused particularly on the repugnance he believed that we should feel at the prospect of cloning humans.

admire above all others have been wrong, and you can give plenty of examples of their wrongnesses if you want. Yet you don't attribute *those* errors to pathology. You don't place *those* people in what Hillary Clinton notoriously called the "basket of deplorables." Why not?

Such inconsistencies are worrisome enough, but it gets worse. Note that this fascinating conversation about why so-and-so is wrong is quite useful in helping us avoid a more challenging question: How do we *know* that so-and-so *is* wrong? That's a question always worth asking, even if what so-and-so believes is that the Holocaust never happened or Barack Obama is a secret Muslim. Just asking the question is a useful intellectual checkup, a reminder to assess the varying degrees of confidence in which we hold our views. (For instance, there is zero evidence that Barack Obama is a Muslim and a great deal of evidence that he isn't, but the secret-Muslim theory is *possible* in a way the no-Holocaust theory is not.)

Here again C. S. Lewis comes to our aid. In a comical passage from a serious essay, he imagines one Ezekiel Bulver, "one of the makers of the Twentieth Century," whose great achievement was the uncovering of this great and lasting truth: "Assume that your opponent is wrong, and then explain his error, and the world will be at your feet. Attempt to prove that he is wrong or (worse still) try to find out whether he is wrong or right, and the national dynamism of our age will thrust you to the wall." So Lewis gives this popular argumentative strategy—"assume that your opponent is wrong, and then explain his error"—a name: Bulverism.*

---

*C. S. Lewis, " 'Bulverism' or, The Foundation of Twentieth Century

It's a variety of the good old ad hominem fallacy, and a very common one indeed, but Lewis is wrong to think that it's a product of the "national dynamism of our age" (whatever that means) or that it's a recent phenomenon at all. It's probably as old as disagreement itself. Consider, for example, one of the most infamous contests of public abuse we've ever seen, one from five hundred years ago: the mutual condemnations of Martin Luther and Thomas More.

But before we consider this case of Bulverism in action, we need to add a complication, a complication very relevant to us: the role new technologies played in it. The intimate relationship between the printing press and the Reformation has long been understood, and if anything has been overstressed. What has been comparatively neglected, in part because it has left so faint a historical record, is the European postal system—though it wasn't really a *system,* and it was hard to be sure whether any given letter would reach its destination. This is perhaps why so many letters of the period were printed and published—open letters, as it were, prefaced to books or published separately as broadsides. But this created an ambiguous situation for any written conversation, sliding along an ill-defined continuum between what we today would call the public and the private.

A valuable tool for understanding this situation is a concept introduced by Christopher Alexander et al. in their seminal book *A Pattern Language,* which explores the social contexts of architecture and more generally the design of spaces. The

Thought," in *God in the Dock: Essays on Theology and Ethics* (Eerdmans, 1970), pp. 271–77.

concept is *intimacy gradients*. Many of the tensions that afflict social media arise from incompatible assumptions about what degree of intimacy is in effect in any particular conversational exchange—the sea lion problem, we might call it.

Everyone agrees that confusions about whether a conversation is private, or public, or semiprivate (e.g., a conversation at a restaurant table), coupled with what has been called the "online disinhibition effect," contribute to the dysfunctional character of much online discourse; but it turns out that this is an old story.* Which brings us to our example.

---

*The phrase was coined by John Suler in "The Online Disinhibition Effect," *CyberPsychology & Behavior* 7, no. 3 (2004): 321–26.

Thomas More's attacks on Martin Luther and his followers, and Luther's attacks on Catholicism (and especially the
papacy), make most of today's online insult fests seem tame.
More wrote to Luther about "your shitty mouth, truly the shit-
pool of all shit, all the muck and shit which your damnable
rottenness has vomited up," and said of Luther's followers that
they "bespatter the most holy image of Christ crucified with
the most foul excrement of their bodies"—bodies "destined
to be burned." Luther, for his part, referred to the "dear little
ass-pope" who licks the Devil's anus, and said of all the popes,
"You are desperate, thorough arch-rascals, murderers, traitors,
liars, the very scum of all the most evil people on earth. You
are full of all the worst devils in hell—full, full, and so full that
you can do nothing but vomit, throw, and blow out devils!"

More and Luther would have insisted that their theological enemies were driving poor unwitting Christians to
Hell and therefore deserved such language, and worse, if
worse could be imagined. But I think the violence of the
language is partly explained by the disinhibition generated by a new set of technologies, chief among them the
printing press and postal delivery, which enable people who
have never met and are unlikely ever to meet to converse
with—or in this case scream at—one another. It is almost as
though they're screaming to be heard across a great distance,
in much the same way that in the old days of analog long-
distance phone calls people raised their voices to be heard
by someone in Paris or Buenos Aires. Rarely will any of us
talk that loudly or that fiercely to our next-door neighbors.

Indeed, one might say that neither More nor Luther can see
his dialectical opponent *as* his neighbor—and therefore neither

understands that even in long-distance epistolary debate Christians are obliged to love their neighbors as themselves. Maybe the very philosophical concept of "the Other" arises only when certain communicative technologies allow us to converse with people who are not in any traditional or ordinary sense our neighbors. In his book *Works of Love,* Kierkegaard sardonically comments, "Neighbor is what philosophers would call the other." And it is perhaps significant that Kierkegaard, who spent his whole life engaged in the political and social conflicts of what was then a small town, Copenhagen, can see the degeneration involved in the shift from "neighbor" to "other."* He is calling us back from the disinhibition, and accompanying lack of charity, generated by a set of technologies that allow us to converse and debate with people who are not, in the historical sense of the term, our neighbors. Technologies of communication that allow us to overcome the distances of space also allow us to neglect the common humanity we share with the people we now find inhabiting our world. For every Megan Phelps-Roper, for whom digital technologies are the means of discovering humanity in unexpected places, there seem to be a hundred people who use those same technologies to *maintain* the Repugnant Cultural Otherness of those with erroneous beliefs.

We might recall here Roger Scruton's commendation of taking "a negotiating posture towards the other"—to do that, I think, is to cease to see a person as "the other" but rather as "my neighbor." And when you do that, it becomes

---

* Kierkegaard, *Works of Love,* trans. Howard and Edna Hong (Harper, 1964), p. 37.

harder to Bulverize that person, to treat him or her as so *obviously* wrong that no debate is required, only mockery. As long as someone remains to you merely "the other," the RCO, accessible through technology but not truly present to you in full humanness, then the temptations of Bulverism will always be right at hand.

LIFE IN RATIONALIA

So this chapter and the previous one have been about how attractions and repulsions affect our thinking. One response to these problems might be to say: Let's eliminate attractions *and* repulsions and make our decisions purely rationally, by assessing the available evidence. We discussed this idea earlier, but our argument has moved further, and on the basis of what we've seen so far, we may now revisit the issue and get a little deeper into it. It's a vital topic, and by exploring it further we'll be able to tie together several threads of what it means to think well.

In June 2016 the astronomer Neil deGrasse Tyson generated a lot of attention by tweeting, "Earth needs a virtual country: #Rationalia, with a one-line Constitution: All policy shall be based on the weight of evidence." This was a tweet likely to warm the hearts of the people who call themselves "the Rationalist community"—people like Eliezer Yudkowsky and Robin Hanson, who in 2006 created a group blog called *Overcoming Bias*.* (Hanson is now the primary blogger there.)

---

*http://www.overcomingbias.com/

According to this model of rationality, which I believe it's fair to say that the people I've just mentioned think is the only model of rationality there is, attractions and repulsions alike are simply biases, and biases interfere with our ability to assess evidence and therefore should be "overcome," eliminated.

But here we should recall our old friend John Stuart Mill's discovery that "the habit of analysis has a tendency to wear away the feelings . . . when no other mental habit is cultivated, and the analysing spirit remains without its natural complements and correctives," and how this discovery led him to a new position: "The cultivation of the feelings became one of the cardinal points in my ethical and philosophical creed."

Mill's point is compelling on its own, which is how I left matters when I told his story. But we might now note that it was, more than a hundred years later, confirmed by the neuroscientist Antonio Damasio, as he explains in his powerful book *Descartes' Error*. Damasio discovered that when people have limited or nonexistent emotional responses to situations, whether through injury or congenital defect, their decision making is seriously compromised. They use reason alone—and, it turns out, reason alone is an insufficient guide to action.

Consider the case of the woman known as SM. SM has a rare condition called Urbach-Wiethe disease, which affects the functioning of her amygdala, at the base of her brain, in such a way that she feels no fear. As Rachel Feltman explains in *The Washington Post*, "SM isn't stupid. She understands what can and can't kill her. But she lacks the quick, subconscious, visceral response that the rest of us feel when we're exposed to danger. In some ways, she leads a charmed life;

everyone she meets wishes her well, and the world is a sunny place. But because she has to consciously process danger, she can put herself into unfortunate situations." Once, when a man on a park bench asked her to come to him, she readily did—only for him to pull a knife and threaten her with it.*

The problem, Damasio writes, is that SM "has to consciously process danger," and human brains don't have the energy to do that kind of processing in every waking moment. If you and I were walking through a public park and a little old lady asked us to walk over to her, we would probably do it without a second thought—indeed, without a first *conscious* thought, because what Daniel Kahneman calls System 1 (Jonathan Haidt's "elephant") would have already been at work establishing our response to the situation, clearing it as safe. We do not pause to work through the likelihood that the little old lady could be a psychopath or part of a criminal gang. We simply approach when called, because our conscious minds are occupied with other things, and we trust System 1 to do the reconnaissance and risk calculation for us. But if some creepy-looking dude who appears not to have bathed or washed his clothes in a year calls to us, System 1 has all its fear alarms

---

* https://www.washingtonpost.com/news/speaking-of-science/wp/ 2015/01/20/meet-the-woman-who-cant-feel-fear/. The woman's story was originally told on the NPR podcast *Invisibilia,* with commentary from Antonio Damasio. In *Descartes' Error: Emotion, Reason, and the Human Brain* (G. P. Putnam, 1994), Damasio develops his theory of "somatic markers": our bodies in a very strong sense *mark* our minds in ways that encode and then trigger certain feelings; these markers are in turn essential to healthy thinking and good decision making. As Damasio strikingly states his conclusion, "The mind is embodied, in the full sense of the term, not just embrained."

primed: we don't stop to think whether to go over there, because that decision has already been made, beneath the surface of consciousness. (The categories "little old lady" and "creepy-looking dude" are positively *loaded* with feeling.) But if System 1 weren't functioning, if it set off no alarms, and especially if our conscious minds were occupied with something else, then we might do just what SM did and mosey on over.

What System 1 does for us is to provide us with a repertoire of biases, biases that reduce the decision-making load on our conscious brains. These biases aren't infallible, but they provide what Kahneman calls useful "heuristics": they're right often enough that it makes sense to follow them and not to try to override them without some good reason (say, if you're someone whose calling in life is to help homeless people). We simply would not be able to navigate through life without these biases, these prejudices—the cognitive demands of having to assess every single situation would be so great as to paralyze us. That's why the English essayist William Hazlitt wrote, "Without the aid of prejudice and custom, I should not be able to find my way across the room; nor know how to conduct myself in any circumstances, nor what to feel in any relation of life. Reason may play the critic, and correct certain errors afterwards; but if we were to wait for its formal and absolute decisions in the shifting and multifarious combinations of human affairs, the world would stand still."

So we *need* the biases, the emotional predispositions, to relieve that cognitive load. We just want them to be the right ones. As a wise man once said, one of the key tasks of critical reflection is to distinguish the true prejudices by which we understand from the false ones by which we misunderstand.* System 1 works on its own, without conscious direction, but it can be changed, trained; it can develop new habits. This is what Mill meant when he spoke of the power of rightly ordered affections to shape the character. Learning to *feel* as we should is enormously helpful for learning to *think* as we should.

And this is why learning to think with the best people, and *not* to think with the worst, is so important. To dwell habitually with people is inevitably to adopt their way of approaching the world, which is a matter not just of ideas but also of practices. These best people will provide for you models of how to treat those who disagree with them: think back to the story of Megan Phelps-Roper, and the contrast between how David Abitbol handled her attacks on him and how the people of Westboro dealt with any dissent from their views. Phelps-Roper didn't just change ideas, she changed communities, and she did so by following certain instincts, certain feelings, about human behavior. (Recall my earlier argument that in thinking about whom to associate with we should consider not just *beliefs* but also, and perhaps more important, *dispositions*.) Before she could have made a rational argument for her change she was already changing, and that was in response to what she saw in the character, good and bad, of the people she interacted with. A model of rationality that can't embrace this kind of change—from one set of biases to another, a set that is better because it draws on healthy feelings—is impoverished indeed.†

---

* Hans-Georg Gadamer, *Truth and Method*, 2nd ed., trans. revised by Joel Weinsheimer and Donald G. Marshall (Crossroad, 1992), p. 298.
† Kahneman and his longtime research partner Amos Tversky made a distinction between Humans and Econs, Econs being the purely

And maybe worse than impoverished. A hundred years ago G. K. Chesterton wrote, "If you argue with a madman, it is extremely probable that you will get the worst of it; for in many ways his mind moves all the quicker for not being delayed by the things that go with good judgment. He is not hampered by a sense of humour or by charity, or by the dumb certainties of experience. He is the more logical for losing certain sane affections. Indeed, the common phrase for insanity is in this respect a misleading one. The madman is not the man who has lost his reason. The madman is the man who has lost everything except his reason."*

---

rational—in the narrow sense of "rational" I have been arguing against—agents beloved of certain strains of economic theory. In *Thinking, Fast and Slow,* Kahneman, summarizing his work with Tversky, explains that Econs are creatures that are fairly easy to understand, but have the unfortunate trait of being purely imaginary. Humans, by contrast, are real but exceptionally complicated, and while they don't behave as Econs do, they are not, says Kahneman, on that account to be dismissed as irrational. "The definition of rationality as coherence is impossibly restrictive; it demands adherence to rules of logic that a finite mind is not able to implement. Reasonable people cannot be rational by that definition, but they should not be branded as irrational for that reason. Irrational is a strong word, which connotes impulsivity, emotionality, and a stubborn resistance to reasonable argument. I often cringe when my work with Amos is credited with demonstrating that human choices are irrational, when in fact our research only showed that Humans are not well described by the rational-agent model."

*G. K. Chesterton, *Orthodoxy* (1908), chap. 2.

four

THE MONEY OF FOOLS

The dangers of too much trust in and reliance on words

The title of this chapter comes courtesy of Thomas Hobbes, the great seventeenth-century political philosopher. Early in his masterpiece, *Leviathan,* he writes, "Nor is it possible without letters for any man to become either excellently wise, or, unless his memory be hurt by disease or ill constitution of organs, excellently foolish. For words are wise men's counters—they do but reckon by them; but they are the money of fools."* Translating Hobbes's point into contemporary English: Literacy ("letters") is an extraordinary invention because of its power to amplify existing traits. By reading, a man already having some wisdom can gain far more; but it is equally true that reading can make a man already inclined toward foolishness far, far more foolish.

---

*Hobbes, *Leviathan* (1651), Chapter IV, "Of Man."

The point should not be confined to written words. As Doctor Cuticle says to some young naval surgeons in Melville's *White-Jacket*, "A man of true science uses but few hard words, and those only when none other will answer his purpose; whereas the smatterer in science thinks, that by mouthing hard words, he proves that he understands hard things."* (*Science* here means "disciplined knowledge.") It is easy to become captive to words, to treat them as though they truly and fully convey genuine knowledge—as though they are real cash money, legal tender, accepted everywhere at their face value, rather than mere counters.

Words are immensely seductive, in ways we don't often recognize. Their power can perhaps most clearly be seen in young children, who become fascinated by new words and look for every possible opportunity to use them. Now, in fact, adults are no different in this respect: we just have learned to do a better job than our younger counterparts of obscuring our fascination, of pretending that a phrase brand new to us has been part of our word hoard forever. *Oh, this old thing?* But we turn the shiny new phrases over and over in our minds, as a miser fondles the coins in his pockets.

The temptation to overvalue words is increased by the role that words play in binding people socially. In Chapter 2 we discussed Jonathan Haidt's argument that "moral matrices" both *bind* and *blind,* and those matrices do that work largely through language. Decades ago the idiosyncratic literary critic Kenneth Burke wrote a brilliant

---

*Melville, *White-Jacket* (1850), Chapter LXIII.

essay called "Terministic Screens," in which he made this point. Whenever we use a particular vocabulary—political, say, or aesthetic, or moral, or religious, or sociological—to describe a person, or a thing, or an event, we call attention to certain aspects of what we're describing. But we also, as long as we look through the screen of that language, inadvertently hide from ourselves, become blind to, other aspects. Burke doesn't believe we have a choice about whether or not to employ terministic screens: "We can't say anything without the use of terms." But for that very reason we need to work hard to understand how our terms work, especially how they "direct the attention": What does this language ask me to see? What does it *prevent* me from seeing? And—perhaps most important of all: Who benefits from my attention being directed *this* way rather than *that*?*

KEYWORDS AND GROUP IDENTITY

One of the primary ways people indicate their group affiliations, and disaffiliations, is through the deployment of *keywords*. This is true across the political and social spectrums, and can be seen in its purest (i.e., most extreme) form in the deployment of certain social-media hashtags: *#RINO,* for example, or *#cuckservative,* or *#intersectionality,* or *#whiteprivilege.* Often these hashtags will be deployed as one-word replies to the

---

* "Terministic Screens" is chapter 3 of part 1 of Kenneth Burke, *Language as Symbolic Form* (University of California Press, 1966).

tweets or posts of others. Hashtags like this do a lot of work, and they remind me of a scene between Humpty Dumpty and Alice in Lewis Carroll's *Through the Looking Glass*:

> "Impenetrability! That's what I say!"
>
> "Would you tell me please," said Alice, "what that means?"
>
> "Now you talk like a reasonable child," said Humpty Dumpty, looking very much pleased. "I meant by 'impenetrability' that we've had enough of that subject, and it would be just as well if you'd mention what you mean to do next, as I suppose you don't mean to stop here all the rest of your life."
>
> "That's a great deal to make one word mean," Alice said in a thoughtful tone.
>
> "When I make a word do a lot of work like that," said Humpty Dumpty, "I always pay it extra."*

Let's take *#cuckservative* as an example, since it's a portmanteau word, and Humpty Dumpty claimed to have invented those: "two meanings packed up in one word," in this case "cuckold" and "conservative." The cuckold, the husband whose wife regularly cheats on him, is, in the classic account, weak-willed, dominated both by his wife and by the man who has supplanted him. The cuckservative then is a self-proclaimed conservative who lacks the courage of his convictions, has become dominated by liberalism, can no longer stand up for truly conservative ideas.

That's a purely pejorative word, as are *#RINO* (Republican in Name Only) and *#whiteprivilege*. But *#intersectionality*

---

*From Lewis Carroll, *Through the Looking Glass* (1872), chap. 6.

is more of a rallying cry. It's shorthand for an argument that begins with one key insight: that someone who belongs to more than one oppressed or marginalized group—a black lesbian, for instance—experiences such oppression or marginalization in a particularly intensified way thanks to the "intersection" of those social forces. To call attention to intersectionality with a hashtag is to remind people of that intensification, but also, often, to suggest that people who belong to various marginalized groups need to see their cause as a common one, to focus on the points at which their experiences *intersect*.

To invite people to political collaboration, or dismiss a political figure, with a single hashtag is, as Alice suggests, "a great deal to make one word mean," and we might be tempted to say that it's a temptation that social media, especially Twitter, with its 140-character-per-tweet limit, encourage. But in fact we do this kind of thing in conversation all the time—as long as we're conversing with like-minded people, friends or colleagues or just acquaintances whom we're confident know the same lingo we do and have the same attitude toward it. "Just another cuckservative" is the kind of thing that might be said to people sitting around a table at a restaurant; or "Come on, people, *intersectionality*."

The sociology of deploying keywords is complicated and fascinating, and not as mindless as it might look to outsiders. I'm reminded here of an ancient joke about a man who is sent to prison, and discovers that his fellow prisoners have a habit of saying numbers to one another—"Four!" "Seventeen!"—and then laughing uproariously. When he asks what's going on his neighbor explains that they pass the time by telling jokes, but they've all been there so long, and with a limited repertoire of jokes, that they've found it easier to number the jokes and just call out the numbers. This makes sense to the new prisoner, so after a few moments of silence he says, "Eleven!" But no one laughs. He turns to his neighbor in puzzlement, and the neighbor shrugs and says, "It's how you tell it."

Similarly, we've all seen newcomers to a social group suffering through a kind of linguistic struggle: they've paid attention to how the group converses, they've picked up a few keywords, but when they try to use them they don't get the expected response. They've used one of the approved words, but not at the right time, or in the right context. There's a curiously *musical* element to the sociology of keywords, a kind of group harmony that develops: the newcomer is prone to missing her cue or singing off-key. It takes a while to find your way into the Inner Ring, and the socially tone-deaf person may never get it right, and may be forever confined to the group's periphery, or excluded from it altogether.

(There's also the still more excruciating experience of using—or hearing someone use—the keywords that mark one group while unknowingly engaging with a wholly different group: a massive social miscalculation that, I assume, all of us have made from time to time. Once I was sitting with my father and a friend of his, two crusty old dudes if ever there were crusty old dudes, and was trying to make conversation with them. I decided to quote a witty comment by Rush Limbaugh—I couldn't abide Rush, but a very conservative friend of mine who liked him had recently relayed the anecdote to me. Though my father never talked about politics, I guessed that he'd appreciate Rush's line; but when I said it a cold silence descended. Then, after what seemed half an hour but was probably only a few seconds, my father lit a cigarette, took a pull, exhaled, and said, "Rush is full of shit." To which his friend replied, "Sure is.")

There's nothing intrinsically wrong with using such keywords—indeed, they're necessary. In any gathering where human beings communicate with one another, *some* beliefs or positions will be taken for granted: we cannot and need not justify everything we think, before every audience, by arguing from first principles. But keywords have a tendency to become parasitic: they enter the mind and displace thought. George Orwell, in his famous essay "Politics and the English Language," captures this phenomenon with an eerie vividness:

> When one watches some tired hack on the platform mechanically repeating the familiar phrases—*bestial atrocities, iron heel, bloodstained tyranny, free peoples of the world, stand shoulder to shoulder*—one often has a curious feeling that one is not watching a live human being but some kind of dummy: a feeling which suddenly becomes stronger at moments when the light catches the speaker's spectacles and turns them into blank discs which seem to have no eyes behind them. And this is not altogether fanciful. A speaker who uses that kind of phraseology has gone some distance toward turning himself into a machine. The appropriate noises are coming out of his larynx, but his brain is not involved, as it would be if he were choosing his words for himself. If the speech he is making is one that he is accustomed to make over and over again, he may be almost unconscious of what he is saying, as one is when one utters the responses in church.*

---

*"Politics and the English Language," in George Orwell, *Essays*

And Orwell concludes that "this reduced state of consciousness, if not indispensable, is at any rate favourable to political conformity"—and also, one might add, social conformity. Orwell is quite right to call it a "reduced state of consciousness": to borrow once again Daniel Kahneman's language, it is as though complex questions that ought to be actively considered by System 2 have been shunted to System 1, where they run automatically. You have to suspect that if you took this "tired hack" to a pub and bought him a pint and tried to get him to defend his position, he would have nothing to fall back on except "the familiar phrases." As Hobbes might put it, what ought to be his counters have become his money, and he has no idea what to do if someone refuses to accept them as legal tender.

THE WORK OF METAPHOR

These keywords are always dangerous, always threatening to become parasitic on thinking, but they do some of their most wicked work when they take the form of *unacknowledged metaphors*. This is one of the great themes of that seminal book by George Lakoff and Mark Johnson, *Metaphors We Live By*. In an especially important passage, they discuss the consequences of one of the most deeply embedded metaphors in our common discourse, the one that identifies argument as a form of warfare. Their examples:

(Everyman's Library, 2002), pp. 962–63. Orwell's essay originally appeared in 1946, just after the end of World War II, a time of great political instability and disputatiousness.

Your claims are *indefensible.*
He *attacked* every weak point in my argument. His
criticisms were right on *target.*
I *demolished* his argument.
I've never *won* an argument with him.
If you use that *strategy,* he'll *wipe you out.*
He *shot down* all of my arguments.*

The identification of argument with war is so complete that
if you try to suggest some alternative way of thinking about
what argument is—*It's an attempt to achieve mutual understanding; It's a means of clarifying our views*—you're almost
certainly going to be denounced as a wishy-washy, namby-
pamby sissy-britches.

We fixate so immovably on this notion of argument as
war in part because human beings, generally speaking, are
insanely competitive about everything; but also because in
many arguments there truly is something to be *lost,* and most
often what's under threat is social affiliation. Losing an argument can be a personal embarrassment, but it can also be an
indication that you've sided with the wrong people, which
means that you need to find a new ingroup or else learn to
live with what the Marxists call "false consciousness." (It was
in hopes of avoiding this choice that Phelps-Roper cut off
communication with David Abitbol, but, as we saw, she had
already crossed a kind of social and intellectual Rubicon.)

So yes: argument can indeed be war, or at least a contest

---

*Lakoff and Johnson, *Metaphors We Live By* (University of Chicago
Press), 2003, p. 37.

in which it is possible to lose. But there's another side to this story: what is lost not *in* an argument but *through* passive complicity with that militaristic metaphor. Because there are many situations in which we lose something of our humanity by militarizing discussion and debate; and we lose something of our humanity by dehumanizing our interlocutors. When people cease to be people because they are, to us, merely representatives or mouthpieces of positions we want to eradicate, then we, in our zeal to win, have sacrificed empathy: we have declined the opportunity to understand other people's desires, principles, fears. And that is a great price to pay for supposed "victory" in debate.

If we look more closely at the argument-as-war metaphor, we'll see that it depends on a habit of mind that is lodged very deep in our consciousness: the habit of dichotomizing. The best—the most accurate and nuanced—description of this habit I know was written twenty years ago by the paleontologist and evolutionary theorist Stephen Jay Gould, in an essay on what he called the "science wars"—yes, that metaphor again. Those "wars" pitted what Gould calls "realists"—"working scientists . . . who uphold the objectivity and progressive nature of scientific knowledge"—against what he calls "relativists," who think that science is but a "social construction" and therefore "just one system of belief among many alternatives."*

Now, the people Gould calls "relativists" would probably have called themselves "social constructionists," because "relativism" is usually perceived as a pejorative word, whereas "social

---

* Stephen Jay Gould, "Deconstructing the 'Science Wars' by Reconstructing an Old Mold," *Science* 287 (January 14, 2000): 253–61.

construction" is a mode of *doing* something. (We're "construct-ing"!) And the realists—well, who wouldn't like to be called that, since it puts you on the side of *reality*. So we can see already that the words people use to describe themselves become a kind of currency, as Hobbes might put it, and a way to make those who disagree more completely Other. Lining up the definitions in this oppositional way puts us already in the region where military metaphors seem like the most accurate ones.

Thus the "science wars" are launched. But for Gould, it seems clear that science is indeed a "culturally embedded" set of practices but *also* a reliable means of getting at the truth about the natural world. Had he left it at that, he would have fallen prey to another characteristic form of not-thinking, the kind that happens when someone cries, "It's not either-or, it's both-and!"—and then dusts off his hands and strolls contentedly out of the room. For Gould, the real intellectual work *begins* when you realize that "for reasons that seem to transcend cultural peculiarities, and may lie deep within the architecture of the human mind, we construct our descriptive taxonomies and tell our explanatory stories as dichotomies, or contrasts between inherently distinct and logically opposite alternatives." That is, we have an inbuilt and powerful dis-position toward dichotomizing—but one that we don't *have* to obey. Once you know that the tendency to think dichoto-mously and militaristically is not just a local phenomenon, pertaining to this or that particular case, but exemplary of "our deeper error in parsing the complexities of human con-flicts and natural continua into stark contrasts formulated as struggles between opposing sides," then you have set yourself a task, not completed one. For now you must try to figure out how these nondichotomous forces work in relation to one another.

Thus, in Gould's case, if scientific practices are culturally constructed but can *also* lead us toward the truth about the world, how do you distinguish between the practices that are really helping us to sort things out and the ones that are leading us astray? This is another version of our discussion in Chapter 3 of bias and prejudice: we're faced in a slightly different way with the problem of distinguishing the true prejudices, which help us to understand, from the false ones, which generate misunderstanding. And that's exceptionally hard work. The cheerful both-ander doesn't know what he's about.

So when people say, "They really mean the same thing, they're just using different vocabularies to express it," or "We all believe in the same God, we just express that belief in different ways," we may with some justification commend those people for attempting to get beyond confrontation, dichotomy, argument as war. But we have to go on to say that the attempt is a facile one. The real story will be far more complicated, and not to be grasped by replacing a fictitious polarity with an equally fictitious unity. Blessed are the peacemakers, to be sure; but peacemaking is long, hard labor, not a mere declaration.

The opposite of the sunny we-all-really-agree optimism is the gloomy we-never-can-agree pessimism. The great nineteenth-century writer Sydney Smith was once walking through a narrow alley (a "close") in London and saw two women, a couple of stories up, leaning out of their respective windows and shouting at each other across the gap between their buildings. "Those two women will never agree," he said; "they're arguing from different premises."* The oft-stated view of the literary and legal theorist Stanley Fish is that whenever we disagree we do so from different, and irreconcilable, premises. So, in a recent interview he gave to *The Guardian* of London, he commented that two radically different accounts of the massacre at the Pulse club in Orlando, in June 2016, had immediately arisen: "In the one case, the case of the *New York Daily News,* the villain was the National Rifle Association, who was practically accused of pulling the trigger. . . . On the other side, the *New York Post* side, this was an event which was one more round in the long-running battle between ISIS and the United States." But these accounts run on parallel tracks that never meet.

> Fish points out that this is true of many communities of conspiracy theorists, those who believe that the Holocaust didn't happen, or that Lyndon Johnson was behind the Kennedy assassination. "The question is, 'Could you show to those people a set of facts that would lead them to abandon what we consider to be their outlandish views?'" said Fish. "The answer to that question is no, because all people who have a story to which they are committed are able to take any set of counter-evidence and turn it back, within the perspective of the story they believe in."†

I've quoted this example at some length because I want to

---

* Quoted in Hesketh Pearson, *The Smith of Smiths* (Hogarth Press, 1934).
† "Stanley Fish on the Impossibility of Arguing with Trump Supporters," July 22, 2016: https://www.theguardian.com/books/2016/jul/22/stanley-fish-donald-trump-winning-arguments-2016-election.

give Fish his due. And his point is a strong one. But it's strong *actuarially,* as it were, not philosophically. It's true that most people don't change their minds. But as we have seen repeatedly in this book, *some people do*—they really do change "the story they believe in." And that's a remarkable and encouraging thing.

We have discussed how keywords lead to governing metaphors ("metaphors we live by") and how those metaphors do a tremendous amount of underground work, directing our responses to others in ways that we're often unaware of. We've also acknowledged that those metaphors can capture something that's true about our human situation—sometimes in argument things really *are* lost—but cannot be universalized without doing harm to our relations with one another. But now it's time to take our diagnosis a step further.

THE POWER OF MYTH

George Lakoff and Mark Johnson wrote *Metaphors We Live By*; the philosopher Mary Midgley wrote what I like to think of as a companion volume, though she didn't intend it as such: *The Myths We Live By*. Introducing her theme, Midgley writes,

> Myths are not lies. Nor are they detached stories. They are imaginative patterns, networks of powerful symbols that suggest particular ways of interpreting the world. They shape its meaning. For instance, machine imagery, which began to pervade our thought in the seventeenth century,

is still potent today. We still often tend to see ourselves, and the living things around us, as pieces of clockwork: items of a kind that we ourselves could make, and might decide to remake if it suits us better. Hence the confident language of "genetic engineering" and "the building-blocks of life."*

Just as Lakoff and Johnson reveal that we use metaphors without knowing that they are metaphors, so Midgley shows that we rely on myths—which are, in effect, stories woven from metaphors—without knowing that they are myths. Organic creatures do not actually have "building-blocks." Similarly, despite what thousands of computer scientists, neuroscientists, and philosophers will tell you, the human brain is not a computer. As the psychologist Robert Epstein has recently written, humans aren't born with features native to computers: "*information, data, rules, software, knowledge, lexicons, representations, algorithms, programs, models, memories, images, processors, subroutines, encoders, decoders, symbols,* or *buffers.*"†

The myths we choose, or more likely simply inherit, do a tremendous amount of intellectual heavy lifting for us. Even more than the empty words and phrases of Orwell's "tired

---

* Midgley, *Myths We Live By* (Routledge, 2004), p. 1.
† Robert Epstein, "The Empty Brain," in *Aeon*: https://aeon.co/essays /your-brain-does-not-process-information-and-it-is-not-a-computer. Epstein continues, "We don't *store* words or the rules that tell us how to manipulate them. We don't create *representations* of visual stimuli, *store* them in a short-term memory buffer, and then *transfer* the representation into a long-term memory device. We don't *retrieve* information or images or words from memory registers. Computers do all of these things, but organisms do not."

hack on the platform," these myths do our thinking for us. We can't do without them; the making of analogies is intrinsic to thinking, and we always and inevitably strive to understand one thing in relation to another thing that we already know. (When we call this process the "association of ideas"—*association* from *social, society*—we're engaging in this kind of mythmaking, treating ideas as though they're little communities. See?) And every analogy helps—but also, as Kenneth Burke reminds us, if it directs our attention one way it also turns our attention aside from other things. To consider the brain as a computer is to ignore its biochemical character and its embodied state—and such a metaphor encourages us to believe that we understand the brain better than we do.

The most dangerous metaphors for us are the ones that cease to be recognizable as metaphors. For many people the analogy between brain and computer has reached that point: the brain isn't *like* a computer, they think, it *is* a computer. ("A computer made of meat," some say.) When that happens to us, we are in a bad way, because those screens become permanently implanted, and we lose the ability to redirect our attention toward those elements of reality we have ignored. Consider, as one final and disturbing example, the belief common in the early modern era that animals were effectively robots or (to use the term of the period) "automata"—"actuated by the unerring hand of Providence," as one eighteenth-century lady wrote, to fulfill the Creator's inscrutable purposes. Therefore when you strike an animal and it cries out, it does not feel *pain*—that is reserved for humans. An action has merely produced a preprogrammed reaction, as when you push a button and a doorbell rings. Therefore one need not worry about cruelty to animals; one actually *cannot* be cruel to them.*

Think for a moment, if you can bear it, of what the consequences of the "automata" theory were. Such is the power of our myths.

So that's the story so far: in search of social belonging, and the blessed shortcuts that we can take when we're in the presence of like-minded people, we come to rely on keywords, and then metaphors, and then myths—and at every stage habits become more deeply ingrained in us, habits that inhibit our ability to think. We can only hope that there are strategies by which we might counteract the force of those habits—and develop new and better ones.

OTHER WORDS

As we seek those new and better habits we should, in the meantime, be tolerant of our inevitable shortcomings. As Daniel Kahneman and his research partner Amos Tversky remind us, nothing is to be gained by demanding that we adhere to a standard of objective rationality that no human being can manage. And deployment of these big prefabricated language machines may be necessary for managing the fire hose of opinionating that online life brings us. But despite their superficial impressiveness of size, our myth

---

* See Keith Thomas, *Man and the Natural World: A History of the Modern Sensibility* (Pantheon, 1983), especially chap. 4.

machines are more delicate than they appear, and our unconscious awareness of that fact tempts us to deal in less than fair ways with the myth machines of others. Take, for example, one of the most common and least appealing defensive strategies I know: what I call "in-other-wordsing."

We see it every day. Someone points at an argument—a blog post, say, or an op-ed column—and someone else replies, "In other words, you're saying . . ." And inevitably the argument, when put *in other words,* is revealed to be vacuous or wicked.

Now, there's no doubt that writers can use words evasively, to indicate or suggest things that they wouldn't dare to say straight out. This is what "Politics and the English Language," that Orwell essay I mentioned earlier, is all about. But often—astonishingly often, really—the "other words" people use to summarize an opponent's argument grossly distort or even invert that argument.*

Even worse, perhaps, is the Twitter version, which begins like this: "Shorter David Brooks," or "Shorter Pope Francis," or whomever the object of scrutiny is, followed by a colon and then an absurdly reductive account, not of what the person actually *said* but of what the tweeter is absolutely confident that the person *meant.*

This kind of thing is closely related to the building of a

---

*Orwell, "Politics and the English Language": "You can shirk [the trouble of clear writing] by simply throwing your mind open and letting the ready-made phrases come crowding in. They will construct your sentences for you—even think your thoughts for you, to a certain extent—and at need they will perform the important service of partially concealing your meaning even from yourself" (p. 962).

straw man. The straw man is an evidently stupid argument that no one actually holds: refuting the ridiculous straw-man argument is easier than refuting the argument that someone actually made, so up in flames goes the figure of straw. And straw-manning is a version of in-other-wordsing. But it's also possible to in-other-words someone's argument not to make it seem that she holds simplistic views but rather to indicate that she holds views belonging to your adversary, to your outgroup.*

In-other-wordsing is a bad, bad habit, but anyone who wants to resist it can do so. (Again, as we have had cause to remember throughout this exploration, many people don't want to avoid it, they want to *use* it to win political or social or religious battles. And again: this book is not for such people.)

Robin Sloan, author of the wonderful novel *Mr. Penumbra's 24-Hour Bookstore,* has described attending debates

---

*A phenomenon closely related to in-other-wordsing might be called "slippery-sloping." If the in-other-worder condemns you not for what you said but for what he insists you really meant, the slippery-sloper says that if you defend *A,* and *A* comes to pass, then *A* will result in *B,* and *B* in *C,* and so on all the way to *Z.* If you say you oppose prison sentences for drug users, the enthusiastic slippery-sloper will ask you why you're in favor of drug-addicted infants—because after all, if people aren't punished harshly for drug use, more people, including pregnant mothers, will use drugs, et cetera, et cetera. The fallacy is common enough that it may deserve a chapter unto itself, but it strikes me as being allied to in-other-wordsing because it shifts attention from what you said and toward something that is at best distantly related to what you said. (If I may be allowed a pedantic moment here: we typically speak of ideas sliding down slopes, but it's really more like dominoes falling, because each unit of controversy is discrete.)

sponsored by the Long Now Foundation. He was struck by the debate format, which, he says, is "nothing like the show-downs on cable news or the debates in election season."

> There are two debaters, Alice and Bob. Alice takes the podium, makes her argument. Then Bob takes her place, but before he can present his counter-argument, he must *summarize Alice's argument to her satisfaction*—a demon-stration of respect and good faith. Only when Alice agrees that Bob has got it right is he permitted to proceed with his own argument—and then, when he's finished, Alice must summarize it to *his* satisfaction.*

And Sloan comments: "The first time I saw one of these de-bates, it blew my mind." This kind of approach is not unique to the Long Now Foundation: it is, for instance, a feature common to the kind of debate subculture that Leah Libresco belonged to (see Chapter 2). But Sloan was amazed to see it in action because it is so rare in the world of argument as war. And as Sloan starts to unpack the implications of this model of debate, he gets into wonderfully deep waters. Writing that follows this model is profoundly dangerous to people who operate within the dichotomizing Us-Them, Winners-Losers model:

---

*Sloan's post is called "The Steel Man of #gamergate": https://medium.com/message/the-steel-man-of-gamergate-7019d86dd5f5#.fgowovsr6. The "steel man" is the opposite of the straw man: Sloan borrows the term from Chana Messinger, who defines it as "the best form of the other person's argument, even if it's not the one they presented."

This kind of writing is dangerous because it goes beyond (mere) argumentation; it becomes immersion, method acting, dual-booting. To make your argument strong, you have to make your opponent's argument stronger. You need sharp thinking and compelling language, but you also need close attention and deep empathy. I don't mean to be too woo-woo about it, but truly, you need love. The overall sensibility is closer to caregiving than to punditry.

It's hard to make this point without sounding pretty "woo-woo," but the alternatives are depressing to contemplate.

Let me contrast what Sloan saw in the Long Now debate with an experience of my own. I am a Christian in the Anglican tradition, and Anglicans have been a combustibly angry tribe for the past fifteen years or so, largely because of issues related to sexuality, especially homosexuality. One day I was exploring one of the Anglican blogs and came across a fierce denunciation of Rowan Williams, who was then Archbishop of Canterbury. The writer argued that not only was Williams largely to blame for the rise of pro-homosexual views within the Anglican world but also he took these unacceptably antibiblical positions on sexuality because he didn't believe in the Bible at all, held no orthodox theological positions, and may not even have believed in God. I considered this an outrageous set of assertions, and defended Williams's orthodoxy, even though I had at best mixed views about his theology of sexuality. And before long I had come to a series of conclusions about the writer's own exercise in bad logic and bad faith, and was hammering out in some detail the views he *really* held but lacked the courage and honesty to state explicitly. But then—in the midst of what would surely have been an irresistibly powerful assault on my opponent's position, and his character—I paused.

I didn't pause because I realized that I was in-other-wordsing with the worst of them. I didn't pause because I realized that I was treating debate as war and was desperately eager for victory. I paused because my hands were shaking so violently I couldn't type accurately. That's how angry I was. So I *had* to "give it five minutes"; I didn't have a choice. And during that enforced break I *did* start to realize what I was doing—what I was becoming. I wasn't offering "close attention and deep empathy"; my sensibility did not overlap with "caregiving" at any point. Now, it may very well have been true that the person I was arguing with didn't practice any of these virtues either. But he was beyond my control. I had a problem of my own that I needed to address. So I deleted the comment I was writing and shut down the computer and walked away. And I have not commented on an Anglican blog since.

METHOD ACTING AND DUAL BOOTING

Robin Sloan's post on the Long Now debates draws together many of the themes of this chapter, indeed of this whole book. I want to expand now on two of his metaphors.

The first is "method acting." The method actor tries to become the character she is to portray, to work her way into that alien sensibility. And yet on some level, method acting—perhaps all acting—brings one to see that that sensibility is not so completely alien after all. My friend Mark Lewis, an actor and longtime teacher of acting, tells his students that the key to playing a really nasty character, and saying and doing the really nasty things that make up that character, is to realize that in different circumstances *you* could be *that person*. Similarly, the life-transforming event in the life of the Soviet writer and dissident Aleksandr Solzhenitsyn came when, in prison, he looked at the guard who treated him cruelly and realized that had their circumstances been reversed, had by some turn of fate he been a guard, he would have treated prisoners cruelly too. Solzhenitsyn, like a method actor, projected himself into the life of another and discovered that they had far more in common than he would ever have wanted to believe.

Sloan's second metaphor is "dual booting," which means having two operating systems, say Windows and Linux, installed on the same computer, so that you can use the computer with either one or the other. If you do this, and alternate between the two systems, you'll learn that most of what you can do on one you can also do on the other, though using different techniques, and in a different style. You won't end up thinking that both are the same, but you won't see them as totally incompatible ways of getting things done either. After switching back and forth for a while, you may find one of them philosophically or practically superior to the other, but the one you like less won't be totally alien to you. It'll be a world you could live in if you had to, even if you don't particularly want to.

And we should notice how all of this is made possible by a format that absolutely prevents immediate entry into Refutation Mode. It's a clever twist on the "give it five minutes" rule: you can speak right away, but you have to speak *someone else's thoughts,* and for that time forgo advocating for your own. It's often said that when you learn a foreign language you haven't succeeded in mastering it until you can *think* in it—which is to say, perceive the world from within that language: and within that language the world looks and feels different than it does in English. Something similar happens when you try out someone else's vocabulary: you experience the world from within that mode of describing it, with a new set of "terministic screens," and some things you're used to seeing disappear from view while new and different ones suddenly become visible.

Moreover, if, as is also often said, you don't fully understand the resources and tendencies of your native language until you learn another one, the same is surely true of moral and political languages. To experience the world in this more complex and less dichotomous way—in this way that promotes empathy and even, yes, love, "woo-woo" though that may be—is to give yourself a chance to think. It is to loosen the hold of keywords, metaphors, and myths upon your mind. It is to demote them from money—the money of fools—to counters—the counters of the wise.

It might also cost you some friends. But we'll deal with that unpleasant possibility later.

five

THE AGE OF LUMPING

*Investigating the categories into which
we lump people and ideas*

In biology, *taxonomy* is the study of classification—the classification of living things. We need to sort them out so that we can think more clearly about them—there are just too darn many of them for us to function otherwise. But it has not always been obvious *how* living things should be classified. Should creatures with wings all go in one category? Those with two legs? But what about birds, which have wings *and* two legs? We are blessed that taxonomy got its start with Aristotle, who, while not perfect, was rather more systematic and sensible about these matters than most would have been.

But even when there's general agreement about what the best system of categorization is, as there has been among biologists more or less since Linnaeus in the eighteenth century, the problems of taxonomy are scarcely solved: for one thing, it can be hard to know when to place something in an existing category and when to create a new one. Charles Darwin thought often about this problem, and commented in a letter that taxonomists tend to have strong tendencies in one direction or the other. The ones who like to put organisms in existing categories he called "lumpers"; the ones who like to create new categories he called "splitters."

These reflections matter not just for biology but for everyday life, because we are all inveterate taxonomists, and go through our days lumping and splitting like crazy. And we tend to taxonomize according to the heuristics— the strategies of simplification that relieve cognitive load— that I've been discussing throughout this book: identifying ingroups and outgroups, deploying keywords, and the like. The hashtags I mentioned in the previous chapter (*#cuckservative, #whiteprivilege*) are essentially quick-and-dirty classifications, Instant Taxonomy.

In general, our culture is a lumping one. And maybe all cultures are. If so, there would be, I think, two reasons.

First, the life of the mind always requires triage, the sorting of the valuable from the less valuable, the usable from the unusable—and in conditions of information overload we start looking for reasons to rule things *out*. Think for instance of those beleaguered college admissions officers, faced with more application letters than they can possible read with care, most of which are indistinguishable from one another, who just need *one* piece of information—a GPA a shade too low, a gap where "extracurricular activities" should be, a grammatically shaky cover letter—to make them feel justified in writing RJ (Reject) and moving on to the next applicant. And even the ones who aren't rejected immediately get classified in ways that might make an applicant feel slightly, or significantly, disrespected: the common annotation LBB, for instance: "Late-Blooming Boy." Even if that's in some sense what I were, I don't think I'd like being tossed into that pile.

Sometimes the need for triage isn't about ruling something (someone) in or out but about deciding what, if anything, to do next: where to invest limited resources. In a hospital, for example, a newborn whose appearance suggests some possible anomaly gets a note on his chart: FLK (Funny-Looking Kid). An elderly woman whose vitals are fading: CTD (Circling the Drain). Someone who dies on the ward is "discharged up" or "transferred to the. ECU" (Eternal Care Unit). Hospital staff make these seemingly callous judgments because time is usually scarce, and doctors and nurses simply cannot afford to pause and consider the relevant in its full human dimensionality, lest they become overwhelmed. A complete awareness of what's at stake is valuable—of course it's valuable, and doctors and nurses know the value—but they keep this awareness at bay because it's not in their immediate context *usable*. Indeed, it can inhibit their ability to do what they have to do.

We use these heuristics, these strategies of simplification, all the time; we just don't like them used on us. We don't want *our* lives summarized with an acronym, or *our* deaths with a bitterly ironic joke. We're funny that way. We don't like our distinctiveness, our *me*-ness, compromised or ignored. I recall a pickup football game I played in my childhood during which a friend of mine received a busted lip.

He touched his fingers to his mouth, pulled them away, and muttered, "Blood"—and then, as though realizing the truly germane point, added, "*My* blood!"

LUMPING AND SOLIDARITY

Lumping is a powerful strategy for information management, and a certain filtering out of individuality is the price we simply have to pay to get our choices under some kind of control. But lumping can also be desirable for a very different—indeed, almost the opposite—reason, as a strategy of *inclusion*. Consider, as an example, the rise in the past half century of the movement in America for gay and lesbian rights. First, people spoke of the common interests of lesbian women and gay men. Then someone asked, "But what about bisexuals?" And someone else said, "You're forgetting the transgendered." After which a yet another person said, "But some of us prefer to identify as 'queer.'" Thus an initialism was born: LGBTQ.

Of course, this was not the end of it. There are strong advocates now for LGBTQIA, in order to make room in the community for those who describe themselves as "intersex" and those who identify as "asexual." Other add-ons have been suggested. But the point is, these initialisms exemplify lumping not for dismissal or ruling out but for *solidarity,* for the making of common cause. The implicit argument behind the idea of "the LGBTQIA community" goes something like this: "We may be a highly diverse group of people in most ways but in one major way we belong together: our sexuality is not treated fairly or respectfully in mainstream culture."

But whenever lumping by solidarity occurs—and it occurs in many different contexts: I could have chosen as my main example some ecumenical religious organization, of which there are many—the unity thus created is a fragile one, constantly threatening to separate. Some feminists say that transgender women don't know what it's really like to be a woman, since they enjoyed male privilege until they decided to try something else; in the eyes of self-proclaimed queers, bisexuals always have an open door to "normalcy"; and so on. Moreover, people might question whether categories of sexuality are the only relevant ones here: black lesbians might note (indeed have noted) that the solidarity that arises from sexuality doesn't make racial difference go away.

Political and social conservatives tend to make fun of this sort of thing—"Ha ha, the Revolution is eating itself"—but their own categories are just as fragile, as the presidential candidacy of Donald Trump revealed. *All* social taxonomies are prone to these forces of consolidation and dissolution, assembly and disassembly, because, unlike biological taxonomies, they're all temporary and contingent—and are often created by opposition. Those who are subject to the same *forces,* the same powers-that-be, can find themselves grouped together, sometimes to their own surprise and discomfort: for example, homosexuals and Jews in Nazi Germany. The various sorts of people who gather under the LGBTQIA banner, give or take a letter or two, do so largely in response to what they call "heteronormativity"; but what happens when heterosexuality becomes a little less insistently normative? In recent years we've seen one answer to that question: some people start questioning the validity of the alliance. Letters get amputated from the initialism, or the whole project of classifying people primarily by sexuality gets called into question.

George Orwell's great fable *Animal Farm* gets its name from the rebellion of the animals against human domination. Animal solidarity is their one great law, their governing principle, and they gain the leverage that earns them their freedom by lumping animals into one comprehensive category and men into the other. Thus their definitive statement: "All animals are equal." But gradually, as the pigs come to dominate, that statement receives its famous amendment: "All animals are equal, but some are more equal than others." And at the end, when the pigs negotiate with the men for joint control of the farm, "the creatures"—all the *other* animals—"looked from pig to man, and from man to pig, and from pig to man again; but already it was impossible to say which was which." It turns out that the relevant taxonomic opposition here is not between man and animal; it is between the powerful and the powerless.

WHO WHOM?

Lenin—whom Orwell satirizes in *Animal Farm* and condemns elsewhere—got one important thing right when he asked a question: *Kto kovo?* "Who whom?" The question has general relevance: Who, we might ask in any given situation, controls whom? Who is sovereign over whom? Who benefits from adopting these categories—and who is victimized by them?

In this light we can see that the creating of social taxonomies is a form of the mythmaking described in the previous chapter. Just as we cannot do without our metaphors and myths, we cannot do without social taxonomies. There are too many people! But we absolutely *must* remember what those taxonomies are: temporary, provisional intellectual structures whose relevance will not always be what it is, or seems to be, today.

Of course, some people govern their whole lives by such taxonomies. And we need to formulate a particular kind of response to them. Consider the example of John C. Calhoun and the college at Yale University named for him. Why, when Edward Harkness gave Yale a pile of money to build residential colleges, did the university decide to name one of them after John C. Calhoun, a passionate defender of slavery? Possibly the thinking went no further than this: that Calhoun was a Yale graduate who went on to become a famously powerful and influential senator and a vice president of the United States. There could have been few better-known graduates of the university.

And Calhoun, when Calhoun College opened in 1933 and for decades afterward, was widely believed to be a great American. Indeed, in 1957 a committee overseen by a young senator named John F. Kennedy named Calhoun one of the five greatest senators in American history. So even after *Brown v. Board of Education* and at the outset of the civil rights era, few people of influence in American government thought Calhoun's pro-slavery commitments were sufficiently troublesome to prevent him from being honored as one of the greatest of senators. Perhaps they thought, *Ah well, people didn't really know better in those days.*

But here I think we need to make a vital distinction: between those who held what we now believe to be a profoundly mistaken view, or tolerated such a view, simply because it was common in their time, and those who were the architects of and advocates for such a view. The general forgiveness of society has been extended to millions of members of the Soviet Communist Party, and the Nazi Party, but the places once named for Adolf Hitler have had their names changed, as have Stalingrad and Leningrad.

Similarly, to those who would excuse Margaret Sanger's support of eugenics as merely a product of her time and place, I say: Sanger did not just "hold eugenicist ideas," as some have claimed; she was one of our nation's most passionate and widely respected advocates for those ideas. It is this ceaseless, tireless, and very successful advocacy for some very nasty beliefs and practices that sets Sanger apart from others who happened to "hold eugenicist ideas."

If we were to apply this same logic to John C. Calhoun, he wouldn't come off very well. Calhoun did not merely *accept* slavery, he was the single most passionate and influential *advocate* for slavery in his era. He believed that slavery is a "positive good," railed against "the fell spirit of abolition," and called those who believe that slavery is sinful "this fanatical portion of society" who wish to perform their insidious "operations" on "the ignorant, the weak, the young, and the thoughtless."

In brief: Calhoun devoted his life to arguing for and

politically implementing a taxonomy that radically sepa-
rated free and superior white people from enslaved and in-
ferior black people; Margaret Sanger did the same for the
binary opposition between those worthy to reproduce and
those unworthy. Calhoun and Sanger did not just *hold* the
views of their time that most of us now find deplorable; they
made those views. They centered their public lives on the
enforcement of taxonomies, and the pernicious myths that
underlay them.

In investigating the lumpings that have shaped societies
past and present, we should, I believe, be charitable toward
those who merely inherited the classifications that were dominant in their own times. But we should be less patient with
those, like Calhoun and Sanger, who pressed to enforce their
preferred categories, to encode them in law and make them
permanent. Such people are immensely dangerous, and for the
health of our public world we need to become alert to the compelling power of lumping: having seen the ways lumping helps
us manage information overload and create group solidarity,
we should become aware of the temptations it poses to us—to
all of us.

THE VALUE OF SPLITTING

So let me conclude this chapter with a celebration of splitting—of the disciplined, principled preference for rejecting
categories whenever we discern them at work. Again, this is
not to say that we can live without them, but rather that we
need to cultivate skepticism as a first response. Though group

solidarity matters to almost all of us in one way or another—it is the stuff of which both Inner Rings and genuine membership are made—on some fundamental level, as Dorothy Sayers once wrote, "What is repugnant to every human being is to be reckoned always as a member of a class and not as an individual person." The key word there is *always*: to be "reckoned . . . as a member of a class" is sometimes useful, often necessary, but intolerably offensive as a universal practice.

Those words come from a brilliant and delightful essay called "Are Women Human?" and in that essay Sayers writes,

> When the pioneers of university training for women demanded that women should be admitted to the universities, the cry went up at once: "Why should women want to know about Aristotle?" The answer is not that all women would be the better for knowing about Aristotle . . . but simply: "What women want as a class is irrelevant. *I* want to know about Aristotle. It is true that most women care nothing about him, and a great many male undergraduates turn pale and faint at the thought of him—but I, eccentric individual that I am, do want to know about Aristotle, and I submit that there is nothing in my shape or bodily functions which need prevent my knowing about him."*

There is a kind of blessed selfishness to this cry—a celebration of the "eccentric individual" who doesn't give a fig about what other supposed members of her class do. But there is also a blessed universalism, a blessed *humanism,* if

---

* Dorothy L. Sayers, *Are Women Human?* new ed. (Eerdmans, 2005), pp. 26–27.

I may dare so beaten-up a word. The Roman poet Terence wrote a line that was once famous: *Homo sum, humani nihil a me alienum puto*—"I am human, and nothing human is alien to me"—and I think this strikes precisely the right note. Terence doesn't say that everything human is fully accessible to him, that there are no relevant divides of race or class or sexual orientation or religion; he doesn't say that everyone else is instantly or fully comprehensible to him. He says, rather, than nothing human is *alien* to him: nothing human is beyond his capacity to understand, at least in part.

Many years ago I spent a summer teaching rhetoric to pastors in Nigeria. The seminary was in a village in the heart of Yorubaland, and many of the pastors were Yoruba, but a significant minority were Hausa, from the north of the country, and Igbo, from the southeast. For me the experience of living and working among them, and thinking alongside them, was exhilarating but also disorienting. Sometimes I felt that we understood one another perfectly, other times that we didn't understand one another at all. The latter feeling was especially strong the day that one of my students, whom I will call Timothy, spoke passionately and at great length about the challenge he had recently faced when a woman in his congregation gave birth to a demon baby. Clearly Timothy wanted me to assess his handling of the situation, but I was speechless. The proper pastoral response to the birth of demon babies did not lie within my sphere of competence or knowledge.

I walked away from class that day reflecting that I simply did not know how to bridge the sometimes enormous gap between American and African Christianity. I was troubled, and after dinner, when evening came on and the air began to cool, I took a walk through the seminary compound and the village. On my return I saw two of my students, walking along hand in hand, as Nigerian friends often do. As I passed, one of them, apparently having read my face, said, "Professor, please do not worry too much about Timothy. He is very excitable." And then he said, as an afterthought, "He is Igbo, you know." To which his friend replied, with a smile, "Timothy is not like that because he is Igbo. He is like that because he is Timothy." And at that moment I realized how utterly my habits of lumping—"American" versus "African"—had misled me.

Terence's great line is a motto worthy of any thinking person. Our social taxonomies are useful, but if we think of them as something more than that, if we employ them to enforce strict separation between one person and another, if we treat them as solid and impermeable barriers that make mutual understanding impossible, they serve us poorly. Our age is so dedicated to its various lumpings that it has, I think, lost sight of these dangers, and of the possibilities that may be found in judicious contemplation of Terence's wise statement. Let a billion eccentric individuals bloom. Even Timothy.

six

OPEN AND SHUT

Why you can't have an open mind, and why
it wouldn't be good if you could

There's a famous and often-told story about the great economist John Maynard Keynes: once, when accused of having flip-flopped on some policy issue, Keynes acerbically replied, "When the facts change, sir, I change my mind. What do *you* do?" The story appears not to be true, alas: no one has ever been able to track down its source. But it's too good a story not to use, and it's always used in the same ways and for the same reasons: to denounce ideologues and to commend open-mindedness.

To be open-minded!—a condition to aspire to. To be closed-minded!—a condition to fear and shun. The contrasting terms are so deeply embedded in everyday usage that they're almost impossible to avoid, but they really should be avoided. They're nonsensical and misleading.

The primary problem is that, of course, we really don't want to be or want anyone else to be permanently and universally open-minded. No one wants to hear anyone say that, while there is certainly general social disapproval of kidnapping, we should keep an open mind on the subject. No one wants an advocate for the poor to pause in her work and spend some months reflecting on whether the alleviation of poverty is really a good idea. About some things—about many things!—we believe that people should have not open minds but *settled convictions*. We cannot make progress intellectually or socially until some issues are no longer up for grabs.

Chesterton said of H. G. Wells—with whom he disagreed about almost everything but remained in cordial relations—that "he thought that the object of opening the mind is simply opening the mind." Chesterton, however, was by contrast "incurably convinced that the object of opening the mind, as of opening the mouth, is to shut it again on something solid."* I like Chesterton's gustatory metaphor: it suggests that when the mind is governed by properly settled convictions, only then can it be truly *nourished*.

The problem, of course, and sadly, is that we all have some convictions that are unsettled when they ought to be settled, and others that are settled when they ought to be unsettled. To understand this problem and begin addressing it, we need to think in terms of the old Aristotelian language of virtue and vice, in which a virtue lies midway between two opposing vices. We don't want to be, and we don't want others to be, intractably stubborn; but we don't want them

---

* *The Autobiography of G. K. Chesterton* (1936), chap. 10, "Friendship and Foolery."

to be pusillanimous and vacillating either. Tommy Lasorda, the onetime Los Angeles Dodgers manager, used to say that managing players was like holding a bird in your hands: grip it too firmly and you crush it, too loosely and it escapes and flies away. In the life of thought, holding a *position* is like that: there's a proper firmness of belief that lies between the extremes of rigidity and flaccidity. We don't want to be paralyzed by indecision or indifference, but like the apocryphal Keynes, we want to have the mental flexibility and honesty to adjust our views accordingly when the facts change.*

All that is difficult enough to manage, but there are further complications: we need to be able to make reliable assessments about the state of our knowledge, in such a way that when necessary we can hold back from taking *any* position until we learn more; and we need to accept that while knowledge may be analog, decision making is often digital, that is, binary. I may believe with some but not absolute confidence that one political candidate will do a better job than her rival, but when I go into the voting booth I'm not allowed to vote 70 percent for Candidate A and 30 percent for Candidate B. (Though it would be interesting to see what happened to elections if such a thing were possible.) Just from these two points we can see what's so naïve about Neil deGrasse Tyson's imagined Evidentiary Republic of Rationalia: it's perfectly fine to *say* that "all policy shall be based on the weight of evidence," but sometimes the evidence is

---

*I am borrowing the language of firmness, rigidity, and flaccidity from Robert C. Roberts and W. Jay Wood in their book *Intellectual Virtues* (Oxford University Press, 2007). Their Chapter 7, "Firmness," is by far the best exploration of these matters that I have read.

insufficient or contradictory, especially when we're trying to predict the future consequences of today's actions, and yet policy must be made all the same. In the laboratory you can and should wait to announce your findings until the evidence is all in and has been carefully assessed, following the best protocols of double-blind testing; but in many arenas of human life, including the political, it's not possible to do any of those things. We must muddle along as best we can, and we must always be honest with ourselves about the muddling, and not pretend that the evidence is more conclusive than it really is. As I've said before: Thinking is hard.

VIRTUES, VICES, AND SUNK COSTS

If we all need, in good Aristotelian golden mean fashion, to steer virtuously between the vicious extremes of rigidity and flaccidity, we should engage in the preparatory exercise of discerning which of those extremes we're more prone to. For most of us, I expect, the temptations of rigidity will be greater, largely because of the informational fire hose we have so often had to consider in these pages. When you are dealing with contents under pressure blasting their way toward you, your natural impulse is probably to brace yourself. You don't want to be moved. You want, precisely, to *hold your position*. It's too disorienting and stressful to be, as St. Paul so vividly put it in a gaseous rather than a liquid metaphor, "blown about by every wind of doctrine."

Establishing and holding a position in that way is natural, probably inevitable, but it can lead to errors. You become resistant to acknowledging that the facts *have* changed; you become entrenched. You've devoted a lot of time and energy to establishing your ground, protecting it from assault. To change now would be, it seems to you, to admit that all that work was for nothing.

I've carried this fortificational metaphor about as far as it can go; to take the argument further I need a new one. Economists speak of *sunk costs* as investments in a particular project that cannot be recovered, and some of them have pointed out that sunk costs have a disproportionate influence on decision making. The more people have invested in a particular project, the more reluctant they are to abandon it, no matter how strong the evidence indicating that it's a lost cause. Poker players who have bet heavily on a hand don't want to fold and lose it—even though sticking with it is mathematically likely, even very likely, to result in further losses. Stock market speculators can't bear to face the fact that their prized stock is going down the tubes, and won't sell at a loss—even when the value of their investment is declining precipitously. Such people are fixated on their sunk costs, on what is irretrievably *past,* rather than on the best available decision *right now*; this fixation leads to the all-too-common reaction to an awareness of sunk costs, what the scholars call "escalation of commitment."

But here's the salient point: poker players and stock investors who don't learn to control their instinctive deference to sunk costs *go broke*. They lose all their money and can't play poker or invest in stocks anymore. By contrast, the average person whose sunk costs have made him so irrationally stubborn that he has effectively reached intellectual bankruptcy just trundles right along, mostly, sustained by habits and social structures that prevent him from paying the full price for his error. There's no reason why a flat-earther, with his commitment to flat-earthery escalated to the max, can't also be a good insurance adjuster. (You just wouldn't want him designing navigation systems for spacecraft.)

In 1954 three social psychologists, Leon Festinger, Henry Riecken, and Stanley Schachter, read in the newspaper about a religious cult whose leader, a woman they called Marian Keech—her real name was Dorothy Martin—was prophesying the end of the world. Keech claimed that she had received messages from the inhabitants of a distant planet named Clarion, and from them she had learned that the world would be destroyed by a great flood on the twenty-first of December 1954. (She received these messages through automatic writing: she felt a tingling in her arm and a compulsion to write, but when she wrote, the words that emerged were not her own, nor in her handwriting. This was the method of communication the beings from Clarion chose to use to warn the world of its imminent destruction.) Those who heeded this warning and joined Keech's group would be rescued by the arrival of a flying saucer from Clarion.

Festinger, Riecken, and Schachter pretended to be true believers in Keech's message so that they might infiltrate and study the group. They had formulated a twofold hypothesis: first, that Keech was a charlatan; and second, and more interesting, that when the falsehood of her prediction was revealed her followers would not abandon her but rather escalate their commitment to the cause.

Whether she consciously understood the relevant psychological conditions or not, Keech manipulated her group in ways that ensured such loyalty to her and her message. She kept the group as secret as possible, and denied access to anyone who could not plausibly demonstrate belief in her messages. As the Day of Destruction grew closer, she made more and more demands on her followers: for instance, in anticipation of the alien rescue squad, they were told to discard all metal items, and some of the women even got rid of the aluminum clips that adjusted their brassieres.

When the promised rescuers did not show up, and the threatened flood did not arrive either, the group was shaken. But then Keech felt once more the desire to write, and the message from Clarion was immensely reassuring: there was indeed a flood, but not a flood that kills, rather one that saves: "Not since the beginning of time upon this Earth has there been such a force of Good and light as now floods this room and that which has been loosed within this room now floods the entire Earth." Because of their faithfulness, they had been spared, and not just the little band of believers, but the whole world! And it was now incumbent on them, further messages explained, to break their habits of privacy and secrecy and to share with everyone, insofar as they were able, this "Christmas Message to the People of Earth." (To which one can only add: *God bless us every one!*)

With every step they had taken over the previous months, the little group—the little Inner Ring—had invested more and more in the revelations from Clarion. They had abandoned families, jobs, social respect. For them the *entire world* had become the RCO. It had become, just as

Festinger, Riecken, and Schachter had predicted, impossible for them to question the validity of their decisions. Their rigidity had become absolute; the immensity of their sunk costs had made them terrified of resuming the work of thinking.

BUBBLES AND BELIEVERS

The book in which Festinger, Riecken, and Schachter recorded their experience, *When Prophecy Fails,** is a landmark in the history of social psychology, but it was not the first study of these matters. Perhaps the first major exploration of the ways people gather together to tie themselves in such knots was Charles Mackay's *Memoirs of Extraordinary Popular Delusions and the Madness of Crowds,* the first edition of which appeared 1841. Mackay explores, with great journalistic enthusiasm, a very wide range of delusions, some religious, some political, some economic, some less clearly definable (the seventeenth-century craze for tulips, for instance). One of his signal examples is the so-called South Sea Bubble. The South Sea Company, devoted to British trade with the Southern Hemisphere, had been created in 1711, and over the next few years people throughout Great Britain, socially high and socially low, flush and more or less broke, came to believe that to buy shares in the company was to ensure for themselves

---

*Festinger, Riecken, and Schachter, *When Prophecy Fails: A Social and Psychological Study of a Modern Group That Predicted the Destruction of the World* (University of Minnesota Press, 1956).

lifelong prosperity. They believed the wealth to be extracted from the countries of the South Seas was close to infinite, the schemes for extracting that wealth infallible. So the value of those stocks rose, and rose, and rose . . . until in 1720 the bubble popped: thousands were ruined and indeed the whole national economy suffered significant damage that it took years to recover from.

Mackay's book was very widely read and tremendously influential: the famous financier Bernard Baruch, for instance, claimed in his autobiography that his reading of Mackay had helped him to anticipate the great stock market crash of 1929 and to sell off many of his stocks. But there's an instructive little coda to this story. In a later edition of the book, Mackay added this interesting footnote:

> The South-Sea project remained until 1845 the greatest example in British history of the infatuation of the people for commercial gambling. The first edition of these volumes was published some time before the outbreak of the Great Railway Mania of that and the following year.

In the 1840s rail companies were sprouting like weeds in Britain, and drew an enormous amount of financial speculation. As more and more of those companies failed, the country's leaders began to exercise some control over the speculation, which led to a crash (though, most scholars think, a far less severe crash than the country would have suffered if there had been no governmental intervention). These controls went into effect in late 1845, though just a few weeks earlier, in October, an editorial writer for the *Glasgow Argus* insisted, with sublime confidence, "There is no reason whatever to fear a crash." That writer's name was Charles Mackay. Physician, heal thyself!*

Most of us will not lose our shirts to perilous investments in a single stock; still fewer of us, I suspect, will give up our jobs and families in hopes of being rescued from a doomed Earth by benevolent interplanetary visitors. But all of us—even Mackay, who made a career of studying human error—are prone to the undue influence of intellectual sunk costs. So in further exploration of these matters, let's move one step closer to normalcy and sanity by looking again at the work of Eric Hoffer.

Hoffer's particular concern, the problem he worked over in his mind for years, was the enormous power of massive social movements, the two most obvious of which in the 1940s were fascism—in Germany, Italy, and (in very different form) in Japan—and communism in the Soviet Union and, increasingly, in China. The more Hoffer studied these movements, and equally large movements from the past, most of which were religious in inspiration, the more he came to believe that they are structurally identical. Fundamentally, for Hoffer, mass movements are a *psychological*

---

*A mathematician named Andrew Odlyzko has written an essay about this incident: "Charles Mackay's own extraordinary popular delusions and the Railway Mania." It may be found at his University of Minnesota webpage: http://www.dtc.umn.edu/~odlyzko/doc/mania04.pdf. I freely admit that I discovered Odlyzko's work by consulting the excellent Wikipedia page for Mackay's book.

phenomenon—however many roots they may have in particular cultural and political circumstances. He called the book in which he explores this psychology *The True Believer* (1951).

It might seem from that title that Hoffer is talking about something quite similar, if not identical, to the kind of delusion Marian Keech's followers suffered from. But it is not so dramatic; it is perhaps even less dramatic than the sort of thing that prompts a South Sea Bubble, most participants in which thought that they and a select number—"we few, we happy few"—were going to get rich while their neighbors sank into poverty or at best treaded water in the social order. The "true believer" of Hoffer's title is someone who belongs not to the few but to the many, someone who strives to bring the entire group (the church, the nation, the world even) within the grip of one narrative, the force of one body of belief, the authority of one charismatic Leader. This kind of fanaticism has no interest in Inner Rings; its movements are extraverted, not introverted. Its energy comes from engagement with the larger culture, not from withdrawal.

The true believer might be said to share the same *ends* as the rest of the world, but has unusually strong and specific ideas about the *means* by which those ends are to be achieved. This is perhaps why the true believer need not live in secrecy and under strict informational discipline. True believers work away in broad daylight, and broadcast their ideas in the public square—unless prevented from doing so by hostile governments, as Christians were in the Soviet Union, or Communists in the era of the Red Scare in the United States.

In what sense then are they "fanatical"? In the determination and resourcefulness with which they avoid considering any alternative to their preferred views. We might consider this point a necessary ingredient of any useful definition of *fanaticism*: No matter what happens, it proves my point. That is, true believers' beliefs are not *falsifiable*: everything can be incorporated into the system—and indeed, the more costs true believers have sunk into the system, the more determined and resourceful they will be. True believers are like the priests in Kafka's parable: "Leopards break into the temple and drink to the dregs what is in the sacrificial pitchers; this is repeated over and over again; finally it can be calculated in advance, and it becomes a part of the ceremony."*

It's important to be careful here, and not paint with *too* broad a brush. Despite what the proponents of #Rationalia might tell you, we all hold with passionate commitment some beliefs for which we cannot provide strong evidence, in any *public* sense of evidence. (I believe my wife truly loves me, though I cannot look into her mind to see whether it's so.) And, as we have seen, it is possible to hold a position too *loosely*, without sufficient firmness. But in general, and on most issues, it's fair to say that if you cannot imagine circumstances that would cause you to change your mind about something, then you may well be the victim of the

---

*The importance of falsifiability to genuine science was first emphasized by the philosopher of science Karl Popper: see especially his *Conjectures and Refutations: The Growth of Scientific Knowledge* (Routledge, 1963), chap. 1. Kafka's parable may be found in *The Great Wall of China: Stories and Reflections,* trans. Willa and Edwin Muir (Schocken, 1970), p. 165.

power of sunk costs. And genuine (if of course incomplete) self-knowledge can be yours if you meditate on just what it is—what beliefs, what social group—you have invested in so deeply.

One of the things I most admire about Megan Phelps-Roper, whose story I told in Chapter 1, is that she did not allow her own sunk costs, which were substantial, to keep her in an environment whose core beliefs she could no longer share. Why was it possible for her to avoid the escalation of commitment to which so many of us fall prey?

Chiefly, I think, it was because social media gave her a way out of her echo chamber. As I noted earlier, you can talk to people on Twitter, but they can also talk back. Every cult, every closed community, controls information flow in order to keep people on message and on task, undistracted by . . . well, thinking. What's fascinating about how most people use social media is that they, looking to fortify their position (to return for a moment to my earlier metaphor), do this work for themselves. They self-discipline, self-control, by weeding out dissonant voices, alternative points of view. But because all the major social media services are so large, with so many millions of users, people can control incoming messages while simultaneously reassuring themselves that there are countless others who see things precisely as they do. Still, Phelps-Roper, simply because she wanted to share the message of Westboro Baptist Church with people who ordinarily wouldn't hear about it, ended up exposing *herself* to people who were very different from her.*

---

*There continues to be a good deal of discussion about how echoey

I wrote in Chapter 2 about the vital necessity of distinguishing between Inner Rings and communities of which it is possible to become a genuine member, and we should recall that distinction now. You can know whether your social environment is healthy for thinking by its attitude toward ideas from the outgroup. If you quote some unapproved figure, or have the "wrong" website open in your browser, and someone turns up his nose and says, "I can't believe you're reading *that* crap"—generally, not a good sign. Even if what you're reading is *Mein Kampf,* because there are actually good reasons for reading *Mein Kampf.* The true believer is always concerned, both on her behalf and on that of other members of her ingroup, for *mental purity.* But as Jesus said, it is not what we take in that defiles us, it's what we send out. And, specifically in relation to what we read, the Swiss polymath G. C. Lichtenberg issued a wise warning centuries ago: "A book is like a mirror: if a donkey looks in, you can't expect an apostle to look out."

---

our social-media chambers are, but recent work by Walter Quattrociocchi, Antonio Scala, and Cass R. Sunstein, "Echo Chambers on Facebook," gives some very strong support to the belief that the problem is real and troublesome. As I write, their article has not yet been published, but a draft may be found here: http://papers.ssrn.com/sol3/papers.cfm?abstract_id=2795110.

seven

A PERSON, THINKING

What English usage and the Democratic
Spirit have in common

In 2001 David Foster Wallace published one of his most delightful essays, a review of Bryan Garner's *Dictionary of Modern American Usage*. In the mode of *Infinite Jest,* the vast novel that five years earlier had marked him as one of the essential writers of his era, "Authority and American Usage" is funny, endlessly digressive, festooned not just with footnotes but also with footnotes to footnotes, and secretly concerned with profound moral questions. Which is to say, it's anything but a "review" in any normal sense of the term. And exploring it turns out to be a vital exercise for anyone who wants to think about thinking—especially if that anyone's ultimate purpose is to think better.*

---

*The essay was first published in the April 2001 issue of *Harper's* under the title "Tense Present: Democracy, English, and the Wars over Usage." However, the editors of *Harper's* made many cuts to what Wallace sent them, and when he republished the essay in his

Early in the essay Wallace outs himself as a SNOOT—his family's ambivalent initialism for a language nerd, a "usage Trekkie," someone weirdly obsessive about grammar and syntax. (SNOOT is an initialism for something, but disagreement about what the initials stand for seems to have been an essential element of the family joke.) Which means that a *Dictionary of Modern American Usage* is pure catnip to him, something to fascinate him endlessly and about which to have a thousand opinions. And watching him spool out those opinions is great fun.

But there's something more universally significant going on in this review that is more than a review, something extending well beyond the battle lines of what Wallace calls the Usage Wars, and the doorway to understanding it may be found in a few sentences from his description of SNOOTs:

> In ways that certain of us are uncomfortable with, SNOOTs' attitudes about contemporary usage resemble religious/political conservatives' attitudes about contemporary culture. We combine a missionary zeal and a near-neural faith in our beliefs' importance with a curmudgeonly hell-in-a-handbasket despair at the way English is routinely defiled by supposedly literate adults. . . . We are the Few, the Proud, the More or Less Constantly Appalled at Everyone Else.

---

collection *Consider the Lobster and Other Essays* (Little, Brown, 2006) he restored what had been cut. It's the longer version I'm quoting from here.

In short, the Usage Wars are a kind of miniature embodiment of Culture Wars in all their endless variety—and therefore a kind of test case for how we deal with disagreement, especially when there's disagreement on matters we care about very deeply. Garner's *Dictionary* came out in 1998, and the fact that Wallace's review appeared only in 2001 indicates just how deeply he got into those endlessly ramifying cultural and moral questions, and the length to which he was prepared to go to pursue them: several prominent magazines wanted Wallace to write about the book for them but balked at how long his drafts were. In the midst of his struggles to get the piece written, he commented in a letter to Don DeLillo that "issues of usage, looked at closely even for a moment, become issues of Everything," from the most arcane philosophical questions to the most mundane practices of everyday life.

But for Wallace the heart of the matter, the most vital extension of the Usage Wars and Bryan Garner's way of participating in them, is *political* and *rhetorical*. "The book's spirit marries rigor and humility in such a way as to let Garner be extremely prescriptive without any appearance of evangelism or elitist put-down. This is an extraordinary accomplishment." Furthermore, "it's basically a *rhetorical* accomplishment, and . . . this is both historically significant and (in this reviewer's opinion) politically redemptive."

"Politically redemptive" is a strong phrase, but Wallace really means it. He thinks Garner is a kind of "genius" because he has found a way to say that certain matters about which most people are indifferent are in fact extremely important, *and* that he (Garner) has the right and proper understanding of those matters, *and* that we all should follow his advice—and to do all this without sounding like a condescending jerk. Without sounding *snooty,* we might say. For Wallace this tone marks Garner's *Dictionary* as an effective book, yes, but still more as a triumph of "the Democratic Spirit."

GRAMMAR POLICE AND THE DEMOCRATIC SPIRIT

Wallace's employment of the capital letters is a typical self-irony, a tiny strategy by which he winks at his own earnestness without actually apologizing for it and certainly without taking it back. He really does believe in the Democratic Spirit, and for him this Spirit is best manifested in the ability to persuade without dictating. Wallace calls the essay "Authority and English Usage" because the fundamentally intractable problem of any democratic order is, precisely, *authority*. When Homer Simpson responds to a command from God by shouting, "You're not the boss of me!" he manifests the Democratic Spirit in one of its less admirable forms, but his defiance does at least have the merit of neatly specifying the problem. Like all SNOOTs, Bryan Garner has strong prescriptive views about English usage, and for Wallace the miracle of Garner's writing is its ability to prescribe without triggering the you're-not-the-boss-of-me reflex. Wallace thinks Garner does this by "recast[ing] the Prescriptivist's persona: the author presents himself not as a cop or a judge but as more like a doctor or lawyer"—someone with demonstrated professional expertise that you're free to listen to or ignore (though with the silent addition if you choose the latter: "Hey, it's your funeral").

If it's not exactly clear what all this has to do with the Democratic Spirit, perhaps Wallace's definition of that Spirit will help:

> A Democratic Spirit is one that combines rigor and humility, i.e., passionate conviction plus a sedulous respect for the convictions of others. As any American knows, this is a difficult spirit to cultivate and maintain, particularly when it comes to issues you feel strongly about. Equally tough is a DS's criterion of 100 percent intellectual integrity—you have to be willing to look honestly at yourself and at your motives for believing what you believe, and to do it more or less continually.

(Which is more or less what this book is all about. I could take those three sentences as my epigraph.) With that definition of the DS in mind, we can turn an important corner in our exposition here, by exploring one important element of this story that I haven't mentioned so far: what it's like to be raised as a SNOOT. To be what Wallace calls a SNOOTlet.

When Wallace quotes Garner's comment that "I realized early—at the age of 15—that my primary intellectual interest was the use of the English language," he comments: "This reviewer regrets the bio-sketch's failure to mention the rather significant social costs of being an adolescent whose overriding passion is English usage." His own experience as a SNOOTlet was similarly painful— and painful in a way that has a bearing on the larger democratic context of the essay. "When his peers are ostracizing the SNOOTlet or giving him monstrous quadruple Wedgies or holding him down and taking turns spitting on him," Wallace writes, "there's serious learning going on"—except by the SNOOT-let. "In fact, what the SNOOTlet is being punished for is precisely his *failure* to learn."

What has he failed to learn? That navigating the social world (especially in a democratic society) requires the ability to *code-switch*.

The little A+ SNOOTlet is actually in the same dialectal position as the class's "slow" kid who can't learn to stop using *ain't* or *bringed*. Exactly the same position. One is punished in class, the other on the playground, but both are deficient in the same linguistic skill—viz., the ability to move between various dialects and levels of "correct-ness," the ability to communicate one way with peers and another way with teachers and another with family and another with T-ball coaches and so on.

And—Wallace never says this explicitly but it is implicit throughout the essay and absolutely essential to his meaning, the impetus that drove a simple book review into such un-charted territory—this failure is essentially an *ethical* failure. It is the failure to recognize other dialects, other contexts, other *people,* as having value that needs to be respected— especially, it's tempting to say, if you want those people to respect *your* dialects and contexts and friends and family members, but perhaps what really matters is the damage this inability to code-switch does to the social fabric. It rends it.

FORBEARANCE

The most striking of the essay's many digressions concerns, of all things, abortion. Why? Because the abortion debate in America is one in which it is obviously, manifestly, universally difficult to maintain a commitment to the Democratic Spirit. Wallace says that some of the things people say to him when the subject comes up challenge his commitment to "forbearance": a moment like that "represents the really outer and tooth-grinding limits of my own personal Democratic Spirit." Everybody's got something like that, something that presses against "the really outer and tooth-grinding limits" of our ability to forbear. And it sometimes seems that today more and more people run into those limits more and more often, on an ever-widening range of issues. This matters because it's when our forbearance fails that the social fabric tears.

The key to strengthening this necessary forbearance, Wallace suggests, and further suggests that he learned this in a very hard way as a result of being raised as a SNOOT-let, is that you have to be *willing* to switch codes. You have to be willing to inquire into someone else's dialect, even, or especially, when it's a moral dialect. You have to risk that impurity. The forbearance Wallace invokes is really a matter of suppressing your gag reflex when you're having a close encounter with our old friend the RCO.

But why should you do it? Simply put: because it's good for you and good for society. It makes you a bigger and better person, and it helps to stitch that torn and frayed social garment.

So why *wouldn't* you do it? To answer that question we simply need to think back to the story I began with, that of Megan Phelps-Roper. The potential costs of learning your opponents' moral dialect are so high. First, you humanize them: they become no longer the RCO, but just . . . people. Remember: *Humani nihil a me alienum puto.* Human beings, like you, who happen through circumstance or temperament to have come to different conclusions than yours. This does not mean that their views are correct, or even as likely to be correct as your own; you need not admit any such thing, but when they *are* wrong they're wrong in the same way that *you* are, when that happens to you (as it assuredly does).

And once your RCO becomes not so O and therefore somewhat less R, you might come to realize that, with a different turn of Fortune's wheel, there you could have been also. You suddenly imagine yourself, though perhaps faintly at first, as someone different from what you are, someone with a different set of what philosophers call "plausibility structures"; and once you imaginatively place yourself within the frame of another mind, then your own views come to seem . . . not inevitable. And this is profoundly destabilizing; which is why Phelps-Roper started cutting herself off from the people who were making stability impossible for her. Instability of this kind—the kind that makes you wonder whether your ingroup is helping you draw closer to the truth of things or blocking you from seeing that truth—is pretty much impossible to live with for the long term. You simply can't thrive in a state of constant daily evaluation of the truth-conduciveness of your social world, any more than a flowering plant can flourish if its owner digs up its roots every morning to see how it's doing.*

And this is why Wallace was wrong to say that "you have to be willing to look honestly at yourself and at your motives for believing what you believe, and to do it more or less continually." You really can't do that, which, I believe, he discovered: his ceaseless self-examination caused him ceaseless misery and contributed in a major way to his early death. Better to follow the principle articulated by W. H. Auden: "The same rules apply to self-examination as apply to auricular confession: *Be brief, be blunt, be gone.*"†

We shouldn't expect moral heroism of ourselves. Such an expectation is fruitless and in the long run profoundly damaging. But we can expect to cultivate a more general disposition of skepticism about our own motives and generosity toward the motives of others. And—if the point isn't already clear—this disposition is the royal road that carries us to the shining portal called Learning to Think.

---

* I stole this metaphor from Francis Spufford, who used it in his book *Unapologetic: Why, Despite Everything, Christianity Can Still Make Surprising Emotional Sense* (Harper One, 2013) to describe the inadvisability of constantly assessing one's spiritual status.

† Auden, *The Dyer's Hand* (Random House, 1962), p. 99.

THE PLEASURES AND DANGERS OF THINKING

In which I explain—no, it is too much: in which I sum up

First, the dangers. I can't promise that if you change your mind you won't lose at least some of your friends—and that matters, because if you learn to think, genuinely to *think,* you *will* sometimes change your mind. It would be easy for me to say, "Well, any friends you lose because you change your mind weren't real friends in the first place," but that would be a facile comment. If you were to find yourself suddenly and completely isolated from your whole social circle because you no longer believe something that all of them believe, you wouldn't be any less lonely because you could mutter to yourself that they weren't real friends after all. You might even come to think that not-real friends are better than no friends at all.

But your fate might not be so dire—and you might not even need to resort to misleading silences or outright lies to keep your social network more or less functional. The key thing will be to avoid displaying the zeal that's all too commonly characteristic of the convert. If you can emphasize all the beliefs and commitments that you and your friends still have in common—and there will be many—while presenting your change of mind on one issue, or set of issues, as something that you have come to with some reluctance and without delight, then you should be able to convince them of your continued goodwill.

At least, as long as you don't think of your old friends as foolish losers. (Remember: it wasn't that long ago that you thought precisely as they do now.) Nevertheless, even if you are kind and forbearing toward them, they may not be so kind to you. It would be dishonest of me not to admit that; but I have devoted much of this book to exploring the power of the forces that inhibit thinking and the emotions they generate, so I'm not going back on that now. I just want to emphasize, here at the end, that you won't profit from this book if you treat it as offering only a set of techniques. You have to be a certain *kind of person* to make this book work for you: the kind of person who, at least some of the time, cares more about *working toward the truth* than about one's current social position.

And working toward the truth is one of life's great adventures. It's hard to talk about this without sounding like one of those Victorian sages—"A man's reach should exceed his grasp, / Or what's a heaven for?"—"To strive, to seek, to find, and not to yield"—but those sages were on the right track, in this matter at least.* There was, in that time

---

* That first line is from Robert Browning's "Andrea del Sarto" (1855), the second from Tennyson's "Ulysses" (1842).

as in ours, an unavoidable awareness of cracks in the old certainties, though of course the certainties they inherited were quite different from ours. The excitement of exploration is what thrills, what gratifies, though not quite in the sense of that old chestnut "It's the journey, not the destination, that matters." Tell that one to parents who've been in a minivan all day with three cranky kids.

No, the journey-destination metaphor is one that we shouldn't live by. Thinking does not have a destination, a stopping point, a "Well, we're finally here." To cease thinking, as Thomas Aquinas explained, is an act either of despair—"I *can't* go any further"—or of presumption—"I *need not* go any further."* What is needed for the life of thinking is *hope*: hope of knowing more, understanding more, *being* more than we currently are. And I think we've seen, in the course of this book, the benefits that come to people who have the courage and determination to do the hard work of thinking. We have good cause for hope.

---

* See an exposition of Thomas's argument in Josef Pieper's beautiful little book *On Hope* (Ignatius Press, 1986 [1977]).

THE THINKING PERSON'S CHECKLIST

In the first season of that masterpiece of television *Breaking Bad,* our protagonist, Walter White, finds himself in a peculiar situation: he has a violent criminal—who goes by the name Krazy-8, which should tell you most of what you need to know—shackled to a post in the basement of the house he's living in. Which leaves Walt with a dilemma: kill Krazy-8 or set him free? Walt agonizes over this decision, and eventually grabs a legal pad and starts making a two-column list. Under the heading "RELEASE HIM" Walt writes several items: murder is wrong, and so on. But the "KILL HIM" column has only one item on it: "He'll kill your entire family if you let him go."

For Walt the making of a list is an immensely clarifying activity, and we should all follow his example—well, in that one respect. Atul Gawande's wonderful book *The Checklist Manifesto* describes the power of that particular kind of list to reduce the cognitive load on people who are already mentally burdened: airplane pilots, big-time investors, surgeons.* All such people must, if they are consistently to make good decisions, keep track of more items than they can actually juggle. Thus checklists: you know what you need to do in advance, so quit trying to remember it all and put it on a list, so you can attend to other matters that require your attention.

Gawande is a surgeon, and though he became a vigorous proponent of operating room checklists, he didn't think *he* really needed them—but then, in the first week that he used one, he and his team forgot important steps three times and were saved by the checklist. People make such checklists for themselves only when forced by experience into intellectual humility; proud people don't want to use them. But once those same proud people *are* forced to use them they acquire a dose of that very humility, because they have no choice but to acknowledge that they forget things they need to remember.

So when I provide a checklist for good thinking, as I am about to do, it doesn't mean that I am going back on my claim, at the end of the previous chapter, that thinking better isn't a matter of technique, and that you need to become a certain kind of person to think well. The willingness to make and use a checklist of this kind is a *mark* of the kind of person you are. It's not a fail-safe method. Even if you use a checklist you can use it carelessly. But if you take the following list and adapt it to your own circumstances, subtracting

---

* Atul Gawande, *The Checklist Manifesto* (Picador, 2011).

what's useless to you and adding reminders of your own, it will help you.

The Thinking Person's Checklist

1. When faced with provocation to respond to what someone has said, give it five minutes. Take a walk, or weed the garden, or chop some vegetables. Get your body involved: your body knows the rhythms to live by, and if your mind falls into your body's rhythm, you'll have a better chance of thinking.

2. Value learning over debating. Don't "talk for victory."

3. As best you can, online and off, avoid the people who fan flames.

4. Remember that you don't have to respond to what everyone else is responding to in order to signal your virtue and right-mindedness.

5. If you *do* have to respond to what everyone else is responding to in order to signal your virtue and right-mindedness, or else lose your status in your community, then you should realize that it's not a community but rather an Inner Ring.

6. Gravitate as best you can, in every way you can, toward people who seem to value genuine community and can handle disagreement with equanimity.

7. Seek out the best and fairest-minded of people whose

views you disagree with. Listen to them for a time without responding. Whatever they say, *think it over*.

8. Patiently, and as honestly as you can, assess your repugnances.

9. Sometimes the "ick factor" is telling; sometimes it's a distraction from what matters.

10. Beware of metaphors and myths that do too much heavy cognitive lifting; notice what your "terministic screens" are directing your attention to—and what they're directing your attention *away from*; look closely for hidden metaphors and beware the power of myth.

11. Try to describe others' positions in the language that *they* use, without indulging in in-other-wordsing.

12. Be brave.

ACKNOWLEDGMENTS

I want first to thank my agent, Christy Fletcher, for believing in the viability of this project when I first mooted it to her, and for helping me shape it into something more articulate and sensible. I am grateful also to the team at Convergent Books for their enthusiastic support, and especially to David Kopp and Derek Reed for shrewd and careful editorial labors. When I sent the first draft to my friends Adam Roberts and Francis Spufford—both far better writers than I am—they responded with warm hearts and critical minds; I am in their debt. And throughout the process of writing, my wife Teri and son Wesley provided, as they do constantly, love and support.

Much of what I say in this book arises from my many years of teaching, and when I think about thinking, the first and chief context for me is always the college classroom. That is why I have dedicated this book to my students and colleagues—past, present, and future—in the Honors College of Baylor University.